**TEACHER'S PET PUBLICATIONS**

PUZZLE PACK
for
Speak

based on the book by
Laurie Halse Anderson

Written by
Mary B. Collins

© 2007 Teacher's Pet Publications
All Rights Reserved

The materials in this packet are copyrighted
by Teacher's Pet Publications, Inc.

These pages may be duplicated by the purchaser
for use in the purchaser's own classroom.

Copying any of these materials and distributing them
for any other purpose is a violation of the copyright laws.

© 2007 Teacher's Pet Publications, Inc.
www.tpet.com

INTRODUCTION
If you already own the LitPlan for this title, this Puzzle Pack will refresh your Unit Resource Materials and Vocabulary Resource Materials sections plus give you additional materials you can substitute into the tests. If you do not already have a complete LitPlan, these pages will give you some supplemental materials to use with your own plan. There are two main groups of materials: one set for unit words (such as characters' names, symbols, places, etc.) and one set for vocabulary words associated with the book.

WORD LIST
There is a word list for both the unit words and the vocabulary words. These lists show you which words are being used in the materials and the clues or definitions being used for those words. You may want to give students a word list with clues/definitions to help them, or you may want students to only have a word list (without clues/definitions) if you want them to work a little harder. Both are available for duplication. The word lists can also be your "calling key" for the bingo games.

FILL IN THE BLANK AND MATCHING
There are 4 each of the fill in the blank and matching worksheets for both the unit and vocabulary words. These pages can be used either as extra worksheets for students or as objective parts of a unit test. They can be done individually if students need extra help or as a whole class activity to review the material covered.

MAGIC SQUARES
The magic squares not only reinforce the material covered but also work on reasoning and math skills. Many teachers have told us that their students really enjoy doing these!

WORD SEARCH PUZZLES
The word search words go in all directions, as indicated on your answer keys. Two of the word search puzzles have the clues listed rather than the words. This makes the puzzle a little more difficult, but it reinforces the material better. Two word search puzzles have words only for students who find the clue puzzles too difficult.

CROSSWORD PUZZLES
Both unit and vocabulary word sections have 4 crossword puzzles.

BINGO CARDS
There are 32 individual bingo cards for the unit words and 32 individual bingo cards for the vocabulary words. You can use your word list as a "call list," calling the words at random and marking them off of your list as you go, or you could use the flash cards by cutting them apart and drawing the words at random from a hat (or box or whatever). To make a better review, you might ask for the definition and spelling of each word as you call it out–or you could call out the definitions and have students tell you the words they need to look for on the puzzle.

JUGGLE LETTERS
The vocabulary juggle letter game is intended to help students learn the spellings of the words. One sheet has the definitions listed on it as an extra help for students who need it or to reinforce the definitions if you choose to do so.

FLASH CARDS
We've included a set of vocabulary flash cards you can duplicate, cut, and fold for your students. Some teachers make a few sets for general use by the class; others make a set for each student. Some teachers duplicate them for each student and have the students cut & fold their own. You can cut out just the words and put them in a hat, have each student pick out one word and write the definition and a sentence for that word. Students then swap words and papers, with the next student adding a sentence of his own under the last one. You can have students swap as many times as you like. Each time the student will read the sentences written prior to his own and then add a sentence. You can cut out the words and definitions separately and play "I Have; Who Has?" Each student in the room draws a word and definition. The first student says, "I have (the name of the word). Who has the definition?" The student with the definition reads it then says, "I have (the name of the vocabulary word she has). Who has the definition?" The round continues until all words and definitions have been given.

Speak Word List

No.	Word	Clue/Definition
1.	ANDY	Melinda warned others about him.
2.	ANGELOU	Her books were banned in the library; her poster picture was in Melinda's closet
3.	ART	Kind of supplies Melinda's parents gave her for Christmas
4.	BIKE	Melinda's transportation to the place where she was raped
5.	BONES	Turkey ___ were part of Melinda's art project
6.	BUNNY	Animal Melinda compared herself to when she was near Andy
7.	CLOSET	Place where Melinda hides at school
8.	CLOWNS	Inspiration for Ivy's art project
9.	COPS	People Melinda called after being raped
10.	DAVID	He invited Melinda to a party after a basketball game.
11.	DONUTS	What Melinda's dad bought on Thanksgiving
12.	DRACULA	Book Melinda read on Halloween
13.	EFFERTS	Store where Melinda's mother worked
14.	FREEMAN	Only teacher Melinda talked to
15.	FRIENDS	Heather told Melinda they could no longer be this.
16.	FROG	Subject of dissection in Biology
17.	GLASS	Melinda held this up to Andy's throat when he tried to rape her again
18.	GLOBE	Mr. Freeman used this to assign art projects at the beginning of the year.
19.	HEATHER	She gave Melinda a card on Valentine's Day.
20.	IT	Nickname Melinda had for Andy
21.	IVY	She helped Melinda draw a more realistic tree.
22.	KEEN	Biology teacher who created interesting assignments
23.	LAB	David was Melinda's ___ partner in Biology class.
24.	LIBRARY	Place where Melinda confided in Rachel about being raped
25.	LIPS	They were scabbed over from being chewed on
26.	MARTHAS	Exclusive group of girls who performed good deeds
27.	MASCOT	The school ___ kept changing
28.	MELINDA	She found her voice in the end.
29.	MERRYWEATHER	Name of the school
30.	MISS	Place where Melinda got stuck for skipping class
31.	MODEL	Part-time job for Heather
32.	NECK	Teacher who was xenophobic, bigoted, and unjust
33.	NECKLACE	Heather's Christmas present from Melinda
34.	NICOLE	She found Melinda after Andy tried to rape her a second time.
35.	NOTES	Method of communication for Melinda's family
36.	PICASSO	Artist who inspired Melinda
37.	PROM	Event at which Rachel broke up with Andy
38.	RACHEL	Melinda tried to warn her about Andy.
39.	SEEDS	Melinda asked her dad to buy these for her.
40.	SPEAK	Melinda did not do this very much.
41.	STALL	Melinda wrote a warning about Andy on the bathroom ___ door.
42.	SUFFRAGETTES	Women Melinda did a report about
43.	TAXI	Melinda's dad's transportation to the airport
44.	TENNIS	Melinda almost beat Nicole at this sport
45.	TREE	Major symbol in the book; subject of Melinda's art project

Speak Fill In The Blanks 1

_____

1. Only teacher Melinda talked to

_____

2. They were scabbed over from being chewed on

_____

3. Animal Melinda compared herself to when she was near Andy

_____

4. What Melinda's dad bought on Thanksgiving

_____

5. Melinda wrote a warning about Andy on the bathroom ___ door.

_____

6. Melinda held this up to Andy's throat when he tried to rape her again

_____

7. She helped Melinda draw a more realistic tree.

_____

8. Store where Melinda's mother worked

_____

9. She found her voice in the end.

_____

10. Melinda tried to warn her about Andy.

_____

11. Nickname Melinda had for Andy

_____

12. Exclusive group of girls who performed good deeds

_____

13. Heather's Christmas present from Melinda

_____

14. Place where Melinda got stuck for skipping class

_____

15. Melinda's transportation to the place where she was raped

_____

16. Name of the school

_____

17. Kind of supplies Melinda's parents gave her for Christmas

_____

18. Melinda warned others about him.

_____

19. Inspiration for Ivy's art project

_____

20. Melinda's dad's transportation to the airport

Speak Fill In The Blanks 1 Answer Key

FREEMAN	1. Only teacher Melinda talked to
LIPS	2. They were scabbed over from being chewed on
BUNNY	3. Animal Melinda compared herself to when she was near Andy
DONUTS	4. What Melinda's dad bought on Thanksgiving
STALL	5. Melinda wrote a warning about Andy on the bathroom ___ door.
GLASS	6. Melinda held this up to Andy's throat when he tried to rape her again
IVY	7. She helped Melinda draw a more realistic tree.
EFFERTS	8. Store where Melinda's mother worked
MELINDA	9. She found her voice in the end.
RACHEL	10. Melinda tried to warn her about Andy.
IT	11. Nickname Melinda had for Andy
MARTHAS	12. Exclusive group of girls who performed good deeds
NECKLACE	13. Heather's Christmas present from Melinda
MISS	14. Place where Melinda got stuck for skipping class
BIKE	15. Melinda's transportation to the place where she was raped
MERRYWEATHER	16. Name of the school
ART	17. Kind of supplies Melinda's parents gave her for Christmas
ANDY	18. Melinda warned others about him.
CLOWNS	19. Inspiration for Ivy's art project
TAXI	20. Melinda's dad's transportation to the airport

Speak Fill In The Blanks 2

1. Name of the school
2. Her books were banned in the library; her poster picture was in Melinda's closet
3. Subject of dissection in Biology
4. Women Melinda did a report about
5. Method of communication for Melinda's family
6. Teacher who was xenophobic, bigoted, and unjust
7. Melinda's transportation to the place where she was raped
8. Melinda's dad's transportation to the airport
9. Melinda tried to warn her about Andy.
10. Place where Melinda got stuck for skipping class
11. Store where Melinda's mother worked
12. Turkey ___ were part of Melinda's art project
13. They were scabbed over from being chewed on
14. Biology teacher who created interesting assignments
15. Exclusive group of girls who performed good deeds
16. Nickname Melinda had for Andy
17. Melinda did not do this very much.
18. Major symbol in the book; subject of Melinda's art project
19. Melinda wrote a warning about Andy on the bathroom ___ door.
20. She helped Melinda draw a more realistic tree.

Speak Fill In The Blanks 2 Answer Key

MERRYWEATHER	1. Name of the school
ANGELOU	2. Her books were banned in the library; her poster picture was in Melinda's closet
FROG	3. Subject of dissection in Biology
SUFFRAGETTES	4. Women Melinda did a report about
NOTES	5. Method of communication for Melinda's family
NECK	6. Teacher who was xenophobic, bigoted, and unjust
BIKE	7. Melinda's transportation to the place where she was raped
TAXI	8. Melinda's dad's transportation to the airport
RACHEL	9. Melinda tried to warn her about Andy.
MISS	10. Place where Melinda got stuck for skipping class
EFFERTS	11. Store where Melinda's mother worked
BONES	12. Turkey ___ were part of Melinda's art project
LIPS	13. They were scabbed over from being chewed on
KEEN	14. Biology teacher who created interesting assignments
MARTHAS	15. Exclusive group of girls who performed good deeds
IT	16. Nickname Melinda had for Andy
SPEAK	17. Melinda did not do this very much.
TREE	18. Major symbol in the book; subject of Melinda's art project
STALL	19. Melinda wrote a warning about Andy on the bathroom ___ door.
IVY	20. She helped Melinda draw a more realistic tree.

Speak Fill In The Blanks 3

1. Heather's Christmas present from Melinda
2. Melinda wrote a warning about Andy on the bathroom ___ door.
3. Exclusive group of girls who performed good deeds
4. Method of communication for Melinda's family
5. Melinda warned others about him.
6. Inspiration for Ivy's art project
7. Melinda almost beat Nicole at this sport
8. He invited Melinda to a party after a basketball game.
9. She found her voice in the end.
10. Melinda held this up to Andy's throat when he tried to rape her again
11. People Melinda called after being raped
12. Women Melinda did a report about
13. Melinda did not do this very much.
14. Melinda tried to warn her about Andy.
15. Store where Melinda's mother worked
16. Part-time job for Heather
17. Place where Melinda hides at school
18. Major symbol in the book; subject of Melinda's art project
19. Melinda's dad's transportation to the airport
20. Kind of supplies Melinda's parents gave her for Christmas

Speak Fill In The Blanks 3 Answer Key

NECKLACE	1. Heather's Christmas present from Melinda
STALL	2. Melinda wrote a warning about Andy on the bathroom ___ door.
MARTHAS	3. Exclusive group of girls who performed good deeds
NOTES	4. Method of communication for Melinda's family
ANDY	5. Melinda warned others about him.
CLOWNS	6. Inspiration for Ivy's art project
TENNIS	7. Melinda almost beat Nicole at this sport
DAVID	8. He invited Melinda to a party after a basketball game.
MELINDA	9. She found her voice in the end.
GLASS	10. Melinda held this up to Andy's throat when he tried to rape her again
COPS	11. People Melinda called after being raped
SUFFRAGETTES	12. Women Melinda did a report about
SPEAK	13. Melinda did not do this very much.
RACHEL	14. Melinda tried to warn her about Andy.
EFFERTS	15. Store where Melinda's mother worked
MODEL	16. Part-time job for Heather
CLOSET	17. Place where Melinda hides at school
TREE	18. Major symbol in the book; subject of Melinda's art project
TAXI	19. Melinda's dad's transportation to the airport
ART	20. Kind of supplies Melinda's parents gave her for Christmas

Speak Fill In The Blanks 4

1. Women Melinda did a report about
2. Place where Melinda confided in Rachel about being raped
3. Her books were banned in the library; her poster picture was in Melinda's closet
4. Melinda's transportation to the place where she was raped
5. Turkey ___ were part of Melinda's art project
6. Melinda's dad's transportation to the airport
7. Melinda held this up to Andy's throat when he tried to rape her again
8. Part-time job for Heather
9. Melinda almost beat Nicole at this sport
10. Book Melinda read on Halloween
11. Exclusive group of girls who performed good deeds
12. Kind of supplies Melinda's parents gave her for Christmas
13. Only teacher Melinda talked to
14. Place where Melinda got stuck for skipping class
15. Subject of dissection in Biology
16. She found Melinda after Andy tried to rape her a second time.
17. Place where Melinda hides at school
18. Animal Melinda compared herself to when she was near Andy
19. What Melinda's dad bought on Thanksgiving
20. Inspiration for Ivy's art project

Speak Fill In The Blanks 4 Answer Key

SUFFRAGETTES	1. Women Melinda did a report about
LIBRARY	2. Place where Melinda confided in Rachel about being raped
ANGELOU	3. Her books were banned in the library; her poster picture was in Melinda's closet
BIKE	4. Melinda's transportation to the place where she was raped
BONES	5. Turkey ___ were part of Melinda's art project
TAXI	6. Melinda's dad's transportation to the airport
GLASS	7. Melinda held this up to Andy's throat when he tried to rape her again
MODEL	8. Part-time job for Heather
TENNIS	9. Melinda almost beat Nicole at this sport
DRACULA	10. Book Melinda read on Halloween
MARTHAS	11. Exclusive group of girls who performed good deeds
ART	12. Kind of supplies Melinda's parents gave her for Christmas
FREEMAN	13. Only teacher Melinda talked to
MISS	14. Place where Melinda got stuck for skipping class
FROG	15. Subject of dissection in Biology
NICOLE	16. She found Melinda after Andy tried to rape her a second time.
CLOSET	17. Place where Melinda hides at school
BUNNY	18. Animal Melinda compared herself to when she was near Andy
DONUTS	19. What Melinda's dad bought on Thanksgiving
CLOWNS	20. Inspiration for Ivy's art project

Speak Matching 1

___ 1. FROG A. Turkey ___ were part of Melinda's art project
___ 2. BIKE B. They were scabbed over from being chewed on
___ 3. TENNIS C. Melinda almost beat Nicole at this sport
___ 4. LIPS D. Melinda did not do this very much.
___ 5. KEEN E. Melinda held this up to Andy's throat when he tried to rape her again
___ 6. IT F. Artist who inspired Melinda
___ 7. ART G. Nickname Melinda had for Andy
___ 8. PICASSO H. The school ___ kept changing
___ 9. CLOWNS I. Inspiration for Ivy's art project
___ 10. ANDY J. Subject of dissection in Biology
___ 11. SEEDS K. She helped Melinda draw a more realistic tree.
___ 12. BUNNY L. Kind of supplies Melinda's parents gave her for Christmas
___ 13. GLASS M. Biology teacher who created interesting assignments
___ 14. LAB N. Melinda's transportation to the place where she was raped
___ 15. MISS O. She found Melinda after Andy tried to rape her a second time.
___ 16. MERRYWEATHER P. Animal Melinda compared herself to when she was near Andy
___ 17. SPEAK Q. Name of the school
___ 18. SUFFRAGETTES R. Melinda warned others about him.
___ 19. MASCOT S. Melinda asked her dad to buy these for her.
___ 20. NICOLE T. Place where Melinda got stuck for skipping class
___ 21. FREEMAN U. Women Melinda did a report about
___ 22. STALL V. Major symbol in the book; subject of Melinda's art project
___ 23. BONES W. Only teacher Melinda talked to
___ 24. IVY X. David was Melinda's ___ partner in Biology class.
___ 25. TREE Y. Melinda wrote a warning about Andy on the bathroom ___ door.

Speak Matching 1 Answer Key

J - 1. FROG	A. Turkey ___ were part of Melinda's art project
N - 2. BIKE	B. They were scabbed over from being chewed on
C - 3. TENNIS	C. Melinda almost beat Nicole at this sport
B - 4. LIPS	D. Melinda did not do this very much.
M - 5. KEEN	E. Melinda held this up to Andy's throat when he tried to rape her again
G - 6. IT	F. Artist who inspired Melinda
L - 7. ART	G. Nickname Melinda had for Andy
F - 8. PICASSO	H. The school ___ kept changing
I - 9. CLOWNS	I. Inspiration for Ivy's art project
R - 10. ANDY	J. Subject of dissection in Biology
S - 11. SEEDS	K. She helped Melinda draw a more realistic tree.
P - 12. BUNNY	L. Kind of supplies Melinda's parents gave her for Christmas
E - 13. GLASS	M. Biology teacher who created interesting assignments
X - 14. LAB	N. Melinda's transportation to the place where she was raped
T - 15. MISS	O. She found Melinda after Andy tried to rape her a second time.
Q - 16. MERRYWEATHER	P. Animal Melinda compared herself to when she was near Andy
D - 17. SPEAK	Q. Name of the school
U - 18. SUFFRAGETTES	R. Melinda warned others about him.
H - 19. MASCOT	S. Melinda asked her dad to buy these for her.
O - 20. NICOLE	T. Place where Melinda got stuck for skipping class
W - 21. FREEMAN	U. Women Melinda did a report about
Y - 22. STALL	V. Major symbol in the book; subject of Melinda's art project
A - 23. BONES	W. Only teacher Melinda talked to
K - 24. IVY	X. David was Melinda's ___ partner in Biology class.
V - 25. TREE	Y. Melinda wrote a warning about Andy on the bathroom ___ door.

Copyrighted

Speak Matching 2

___ 1. LIBRARY
___ 2. MARTHAS
___ 3. STALL
___ 4. MODEL
___ 5. IT
___ 6. BONES
___ 7. FREEMAN
___ 8. KEEN
___ 9. FRIENDS
___ 10. PICASSO
___ 11. LIPS
___ 12. MISS
___ 13. GLOBE
___ 14. GLASS
___ 15. RACHEL
___ 16. EFFERTS
___ 17. DAVID
___ 18. HEATHER
___ 19. TREE
___ 20. PROM
___ 21. COPS
___ 22. ANDY
___ 23. NECK
___ 24. MERRYWEATHER
___ 25. CLOSET

A. Heather told Melinda they could no longer be this.
B. Teacher who was xenophobic, bigoted, and unjust
C. Event at which Rachel broke up with Andy
D. Nickname Melinda had for Andy
E. Part-time job for Heather
F. He invited Melinda to a party after a basketball game.
G. People Melinda called after being raped
H. Store where Melinda's mother worked
I. They were scabbed over from being chewed on
J. Only teacher Melinda talked to
K. Place where Melinda got stuck for skipping class
L. Melinda wrote a warning about Andy on the bathroom ___ door.
M. Major symbol in the book; subject of Melinda's art project
N. Exclusive group of girls who performed good deeds
O. Melinda warned others about him.
P. Name of the school
Q. Turkey ___ were part of Melinda's art project
R. Place where Melinda hides at school
S. She gave Melinda a card on Valentine's Day.
T. Place where Melinda confided in Rachel about being raped
U. Melinda tried to warn her about Andy.
V. Biology teacher who created interesting assignments
W. Artist who inspired Melinda
X. Melinda held this up to Andy's throat when he tried to rape her again
Y. Mr. Freeman used this to assign art projects at the beginning of the year.

Speak Matching 2 Answer Key

T - 1.	LIBRARY	A.	Heather told Melinda they could no longer be this.
N - 2.	MARTHAS	B.	Teacher who was xenophobic, bigoted, and unjust
L - 3.	STALL	C.	Event at which Rachel broke up with Andy
E - 4.	MODEL	D.	Nickname Melinda had for Andy
D - 5.	IT	E.	Part-time job for Heather
Q - 6.	BONES	F.	He invited Melinda to a party after a basketball game.
J - 7.	FREEMAN	G.	People Melinda called after being raped
V - 8.	KEEN	H.	Store where Melinda's mother worked
A - 9.	FRIENDS	I.	They were scabbed over from being chewed on
W - 10.	PICASSO	J.	Only teacher Melinda talked to
I - 11.	LIPS	K.	Place where Melinda got stuck for skipping class
K - 12.	MISS	L.	Melinda wrote a warning about Andy on the bathroom ___ door.
Y - 13.	GLOBE	M.	Major symbol in the book; subject of Melinda's art project
X - 14.	GLASS	N.	Exclusive group of girls who performed good deeds
U - 15.	RACHEL	O.	Melinda warned others about him.
H - 16.	EFFERTS	P.	Name of the school
F - 17.	DAVID	Q.	Turkey ___ were part of Melinda's art project
S - 18.	HEATHER	R.	Place where Melinda hides at school
M - 19.	TREE	S.	She gave Melinda a card on Valentine's Day.
C - 20.	PROM	T.	Place where Melinda confided in Rachel about being raped
G - 21.	COPS	U.	Melinda tried to warn her about Andy.
O - 22.	ANDY	V.	Biology teacher who created interesting assignments
B - 23.	NECK	W.	Artist who inspired Melinda
P - 24.	MERRYWEATHER	X.	Melinda held this up to Andy's throat when he tried to rape her again
R - 25.	CLOSET	Y.	Mr. Freeman used this to assign art projects at the beginning of the year.

Speak Matching 3

___ 1. FRIENDS
___ 2. GLASS
___ 3. STALL
___ 4. ANDY
___ 5. DRACULA
___ 6. MASCOT
___ 7. IVY
___ 8. MERRYWEATHER
___ 9. TENNIS
___ 10. CLOWNS
___ 11. LAB
___ 12. SUFFRAGETTES
___ 13. MELINDA
___ 14. NECKLACE
___ 15. PROM
___ 16. HEATHER
___ 17. TAXI
___ 18. SPEAK
___ 19. CLOSET
___ 20. FREEMAN
___ 21. FROG
___ 22. NECK
___ 23. COPS
___ 24. DAVID
___ 25. LIPS

A. Melinda held this up to Andy's throat when he tried to rape her again
B. Melinda's dad's transportation to the airport
C. Event at which Rachel broke up with Andy
D. Melinda did not do this very much.
E. Women Melinda did a report about
F. Book Melinda read on Halloween
G. Melinda warned others about him.
H. Subject of dissection in Biology
I. Teacher who was xenophobic, bigoted, and unjust
J. Name of the school
K. They were scabbed over from being chewed on
L. Inspiration for Ivy's art project
M. Heather's Christmas present from Melinda
N. Place where Melinda hides at school
O. Heather told Melinda they could no longer be this.
P. He invited Melinda to a party after a basketball game.
Q. Melinda wrote a warning about Andy on the bathroom ___ door.
R. David was Melinda's ___ partner in Biology class.
S. Only teacher Melinda talked to
T. People Melinda called after being raped
U. Melinda almost beat Nicole at this sport
V. She found her voice in the end.
W. The school ___ kept changing
X. She gave Melinda a card on Valentine's Day.
Y. She helped Melinda draw a more realistic tree.

Speak Matching 3 Answer Key

O - 1. FRIENDS	A. Melinda held this up to Andy's throat when he tried to rape her again
A - 2. GLASS	B. Melinda's dad's transportation to the airport
Q - 3. STALL	C. Event at which Rachel broke up with Andy
G - 4. ANDY	D. Melinda did not do this very much.
F - 5. DRACULA	E. Women Melinda did a report about
W - 6. MASCOT	F. Book Melinda read on Halloween
Y - 7. IVY	G. Melinda warned others about him.
J - 8. MERRYWEATHER	H. Subject of dissection in Biology
U - 9. TENNIS	I. Teacher who was xenophobic, bigoted, and unjust
L - 10. CLOWNS	J. Name of the school
R - 11. LAB	K. They were scabbed over from being chewed on
E - 12. SUFFRAGETTES	L. Inspiration for Ivy's art project
V - 13. MELINDA	M. Heather's Christmas present from Melinda
M - 14. NECKLACE	N. Place where Melinda hides at school
C - 15. PROM	O. Heather told Melinda they could no longer be this.
X - 16. HEATHER	P. He invited Melinda to a party after a basketball game.
B - 17. TAXI	Q. Melinda wrote a warning about Andy on the bathroom ___ door.
D - 18. SPEAK	R. David was Melinda's ___ partner in Biology class.
N - 19. CLOSET	S. Only teacher Melinda talked to
S - 20. FREEMAN	T. People Melinda called after being raped
H - 21. FROG	U. Melinda almost beat Nicole at this sport
I - 22. NECK	V. She found her voice in the end.
T - 23. COPS	W. The school ___ kept changing
P - 24. DAVID	X. She gave Melinda a card on Valentine's Day.
K - 25. LIPS	Y. She helped Melinda draw a more realistic tree.

Speak Matching 4

___ 1. MASCOT
___ 2. NOTES
___ 3. LIPS
___ 4. MERRYWEATHER
___ 5. CLOWNS
___ 6. TREE
___ 7. PICASSO
___ 8. TENNIS
___ 9. COPS
___ 10. GLOBE
___ 11. BONES
___ 12. HEATHER
___ 13. STALL
___ 14. RACHEL
___ 15. SEEDS
___ 16. LAB
___ 17. BIKE
___ 18. SUFFRAGETTES
___ 19. MODEL
___ 20. NECK
___ 21. TAXI
___ 22. CLOSET
___ 23. ANGELOU
___ 24. MISS
___ 25. IT

A. Melinda wrote a warning about Andy on the bathroom ___ door.
B. Her books were banned in the library; her poster picture was in Melinda's closet
C. Artist who inspired Melinda
D. Inspiration for Ivy's art project
E. She gave Melinda a card on Valentine's Day.
F. Melinda's transportation to the place where she was raped
G. Place where Melinda hides at school
H. Nickname Melinda had for Andy
I. They were scabbed over from being chewed on
J. The school ___ kept changing
K. Teacher who was xenophobic, bigoted, and unjust
L. Mr. Freeman used this to assign art projects at the beginning of the year.
M. Melinda's dad's transportation to the airport
N. Melinda tried to warn her about Andy.
O. Melinda asked her dad to buy these for her.
P. Women Melinda did a report about
Q. Turkey ___ were part of Melinda's art project
R. People Melinda called after being raped
S. Major symbol in the book; subject of Melinda's art project
T. Part-time job for Heather
U. Melinda almost beat Nicole at this sport
V. Method of communication for Melinda's family
W. David was Melinda's ___ partner in Biology class.
X. Name of the school
Y. Place where Melinda got stuck for skipping class

Speak Matching 4 Answer Key

J - 1. MASCOT	A. Melinda wrote a warning about Andy on the bathroom ___ door.
V - 2. NOTES	B. Her books were banned in the library; her poster picture was in Melinda's closet
I - 3. LIPS	C. Artist who inspired Melinda
X - 4. MERRYWEATHER	D. Inspiration for Ivy's art project
D - 5. CLOWNS	E. She gave Melinda a card on Valentine's Day.
S - 6. TREE	F. Melinda's transportation to the place where she was raped
C - 7. PICASSO	G. Place where Melinda hides at school
U - 8. TENNIS	H. Nickname Melinda had for Andy
R - 9. COPS	I. They were scabbed over from being chewed on
L - 10. GLOBE	J. The school ___ kept changing
Q - 11. BONES	K. Teacher who was xenophobic, bigoted, and unjust
E - 12. HEATHER	L. Mr. Freeman used this to assign art projects at the beginning of the year.
A - 13. STALL	M. Melinda's dad's transportation to the airport
N - 14. RACHEL	N. Melinda tried to warn her about Andy.
O - 15. SEEDS	O. Melinda asked her dad to buy these for her.
W - 16. LAB	P. Women Melinda did a report about
F - 17. BIKE	Q. Turkey ___ were part of Melinda's art project
P - 18. SUFFRAGETTES	R. People Melinda called after being raped
T - 19. MODEL	S. Major symbol in the book; subject of Melinda's art project
K - 20. NECK	T. Part-time job for Heather
M - 21. TAXI	U. Melinda almost beat Nicole at this sport
G - 22. CLOSET	V. Method of communication for Melinda's family
B - 23. ANGELOU	W. David was Melinda's ___ partner in Biology class.
Y - 24. MISS	X. Name of the school
H - 25. IT	Y. Place where Melinda got stuck for skipping class

Speak Magic Squares 1

Match the definition with the vocabulary word. Put your answers in the magic squares below. When your answers are correct, all columns and rows will add to the same number.

A. FRIENDS
B. BIKE
C. HEATHER
D. SPEAK
E. MELINDA
F. LAB
G. ANGELOU
H. DAVID
I. STALL
J. TENNIS
K. FROG
L. SEEDS
M. MASCOT
N. LIBRARY
O. LIPS
P. DONUTS

1. He invited Melinda to a party after a basketball game.
2. The school ___ kept changing
3. Melinda's transportation to the place where she was raped
4. Subject of dissection in Biology
5. Melinda almost beat Nicole at this sport
6. She gave Melinda a card on Valentine's Day.
7. What Melinda's dad bought on Thanksgiving
8. She found her voice in the end.
9. They were scabbed over from being chewed on
10. David was Melinda's ___ partner in Biology class.
11. Melinda wrote a warning about Andy on the bathroom ___ door.
12. Melinda did not do this very much.
13. Heather told Melinda they could no longer be this.
14. Melinda asked her dad to buy these for her.
15. Her books were banned in the library; her poster picture was in Melinda's closet
16. Place where Melinda confided in Rachel about being raped

A=	B=	C=	D=
E=	F=	G=	H=
I=	J=	K=	L=
M=	N=	O=	P=

Speak Magic Squares 1 Answer Key

Match the definition with the vocabulary word. Put your answers in the magic squares below. When your answers are correct, all columns and rows will add to the same number.

A. FRIENDS
B. BIKE
C. HEATHER
D. SPEAK
E. MELINDA
F. LAB
G. ANGELOU
H. DAVID
I. STALL
J. TENNIS
K. FROG
L. SEEDS
M. MASCOT
N. LIBRARY
O. LIPS
P. DONUTS

1. He invited Melinda to a party after a basketball game.
2. The school ___ kept changing
3. Melinda's transportation to the place where she was raped
4. Subject of dissection in Biology
5. Melinda almost beat Nicole at this sport
6. She gave Melinda a card on Valentine's Day.
7. What Melinda's dad bought on Thanksgiving
8. She found her voice in the end.
9. They were scabbed over from being chewed on
10. David was Melinda's ___ partner in Biology class.
11. Melinda wrote a warning about Andy on the bathroom ___ door.
12. Melinda did not do this very much.
13. Heather told Melinda they could no longer be this.
14. Melinda asked her dad to buy these for her.
15. Her books were banned in the library; her poster picture was in Melinda's closet
16. Place where Melinda confided in Rachel about being raped

A=13	B=3	C=6	D=12
E=8	F=10	G=15	H=1
I=11	J=5	K=4	L=14
M=2	N=16	O=9	P=7

Speak Magic Squares 2

Match the definition with the vocabulary word. Put your answers in the magic squares below. When your answers are correct, all columns and rows will add to the same number.

A. TREE
B. RACHEL
C. NOTES
D. TAXI
E. TENNIS
F. MASCOT
G. IVY
H. MELINDA
I. MARTHAS
J. SPEAK
K. BUNNY
L. CLOSET
M. IT
N. SEEDS
O. MERRYWEATHER
P. KEEN

1. Melinda asked her dad to buy these for her.
2. She helped Melinda draw a more realistic tree.
3. Place where Melinda hides at school
4. Major symbol in the book; subject of Melinda's art project
5. Animal Melinda compared herself to when she was near Andy
6. Melinda tried to warn her about Andy.
7. Nickname Melinda had for Andy
8. She found her voice in the end.
9. Melinda almost beat Nicole at this sport
10. Biology teacher who created interesting assignments
11. Method of communication for Melinda's family
12. Melinda did not do this very much.
13. Melinda's dad's transportation to the airport
14. Exclusive group of girls who performed good deeds
15. The school ___ kept changing
16. Name of the school

A=	B=	C=	D=
E=	F=	G=	H=
I=	J=	K=	L=
M=	N=	O=	P=

Speak Magic Squares 2 Answer Key

Match the definition with the vocabulary word. Put your answers in the magic squares below. When your answers are correct, all columns and rows will add to the same number.

A. TREE
B. RACHEL
C. NOTES
D. TAXI
E. TENNIS
F. MASCOT
G. IVY
H. MELINDA
I. MARTHAS
J. SPEAK
K. BUNNY
L. CLOSET
M. IT
N. SEEDS
O. MERRYWEATHER
P. KEEN

1. Melinda asked her dad to buy these for her.
2. She helped Melinda draw a more realistic tree.
3. Place where Melinda hides at school
4. Major symbol in the book; subject of Melinda's art project
5. Animal Melinda compared herself to when she was near Andy
6. Melinda tried to warn her about Andy.
7. Nickname Melinda had for Andy
8. She found her voice in the end.
9. Melinda almost beat Nicole at this sport
10. Biology teacher who created interesting assignments
11. Method of communication for Melinda's family
12. Melinda did not do this very much.
13. Melinda's dad's transportation to the airport
14. Exclusive group of girls who performed good deeds
15. The school ___ kept changing
16. Name of the school

A=4	B=6	C=11	D=13
E=9	F=15	G=2	H=8
I=14	J=12	K=5	L=3
M=7	N=1	O=16	P=10

Speak Magic Squares 3

Match the definition with the vocabulary word. Put your answers in the magic squares below. When your answers are correct, all columns and rows will add to the same number.

A. RACHEL
B. ANGELOU
C. MASCOT
D. SUFFRAGETTES
E. NICOLE
F. FRIENDS
G. TENNIS
H. LAB
I. BUNNY
J. COPS
K. MARTHAS
L. MERRYWEATHER
M. BIKE
N. NECK
O. TREE
P. FROG

1. Melinda's transportation to the place where she was raped
2. Heather told Melinda they could no longer be this.
3. David was Melinda's ___ partner in Biology class.
4. Major symbol in the book; subject of Melinda's art project
5. Name of the school
6. The school ___ kept changing
7. Melinda tried to warn her about Andy.
8. People Melinda called after being raped
9. Exclusive group of girls who performed good deeds
10. Women Melinda did a report about
11. Her books were banned in the library; her poster picture was in Melinda's closet
12. Animal Melinda compared herself to when she was near Andy
13. Teacher who was xenophobic, bigoted, and unjust
14. She found Melinda after Andy tried to rape her a second time.
15. Melinda almost beat Nicole at this sport
16. Subject of dissection in Biology

A=	B=	C=	D=
E=	F=	G=	H=
I=	J=	K=	L=
M=	N=	O=	P=

25
Copyrighted

Speak Magic Squares 3 Answer Key

Match the definition with the vocabulary word. Put your answers in the magic squares below. When your answers are correct, all columns and rows will add to the same number.

A. RACHEL
B. ANGELOU
C. MASCOT
D. SUFFRAGETTES
E. NICOLE
F. FRIENDS
G. TENNIS
H. LAB
I. BUNNY
J. COPS
K. MARTHAS
L. MERRYWEATHER
M. BIKE
N. NECK
O. TREE
P. FROG

1. Melinda's transportation to the place where she was raped
2. Heather told Melinda they could no longer be this.
3. David was Melinda's ___ partner in Biology class.
4. Major symbol in the book; subject of Melinda's art project
5. Name of the school
6. The school ___ kept changing
7. Melinda tried to warn her about Andy.
8. People Melinda called after being raped
9. Exclusive group of girls who performed good deeds
10. Women Melinda did a report about
11. Her books were banned in the library; her poster picture was in Melinda's closet
12. Animal Melinda compared herself to when she was near Andy
13. Teacher who was xenophobic, bigoted, and unjust
14. She found Melinda after Andy tried to rape her a second time.
15. Melinda almost beat Nicole at this sport
16. Subject of dissection in Biology

A=7	B=11	C=6	D=10
E=14	F=2	G=15	H=3
I=12	J=8	K=9	L=5
M=1	N=13	O=4	P=16

Speak Magic Squares 4

Match the definition with the vocabulary word. Put your answers in the magic squares below. When your answers are correct, all columns and rows will add to the same number.

A. IT
B. MARTHAS
C. TENNIS
D. MISS
E. DRACULA
F. STALL
G. ANDY
H. NOTES
I. HEATHER
J. SUFFRAGETTES
K. COPS
L. GLOBE
M. TAXI
N. GLASS
O. ART
P. PROM

1. Method of communication for Melinda's family
2. Nickname Melinda had for Andy
3. Exclusive group of girls who performed good deeds
4. Melinda warned others about him.
5. Women Melinda did a report about
6. Kind of supplies Melinda's parents gave her for Christmas
7. Event at which Rachel broke up with Andy
8. She gave Melinda a card on Valentine's Day.
9. People Melinda called after being raped
10. Melinda held this up to Andy's throat when he tried to rape her again
11. Melinda's dad's transportation to the airport
12. Mr. Freeman used this to assign art projects at the beginning of the year.
13. Book Melinda read on Halloween
14. Place where Melinda got stuck for skipping class
15. Melinda almost beat Nicole at this sport
16. Melinda wrote a warning about Andy on the bathroom ___ door.

A=	B=	C=	D=
E=	F=	G=	H=
I=	J=	K=	L=
M=	N=	O=	P=

Speak Magic Squares 4 Answer Key

Match the definition with the vocabulary word. Put your answers in the magic squares below. When your answers are correct, all columns and rows will add to the same number.

A. IT
B. MARTHAS
C. TENNIS
D. MISS
E. DRACULA
F. STALL
G. ANDY
H. NOTES
I. HEATHER
J. SUFFRAGETTES
K. COPS
L. GLOBE
M. TAXI
N. GLASS
O. ART
P. PROM

1. Method of communication for Melinda's family
2. Nickname Melinda had for Andy
3. Exclusive group of girls who performed good deeds
4. Melinda warned others about him.
5. Women Melinda did a report about
6. Kind of supplies Melinda's parents gave her for Christmas
7. Event at which Rachel broke up with Andy
8. She gave Melinda a card on Valentine's Day.
9. People Melinda called after being raped
10. Melinda held this up to Andy's throat when he tried to rape her again
11. Melinda's dad's transportation to the airport
12. Mr. Freeman used this to assign art projects at the beginning of the year.
13. Book Melinda read on Halloween
14. Place where Melinda got stuck for skipping class
15. Melinda almost beat Nicole at this sport
16. Melinda wrote a warning about Andy on the bathroom ___ door.

A=2	B=3	C=15	D=14
E=13	F=16	G=4	H=1
I=8	J=5	K=9	L=12
M=11	N=10	O=6	P=7

Speak Word Search 1

```
M A R T H A S N G T I K L I P S B S G Q
E B Z Q X H T O R L A Q A D Y P P T L W
R N R C Y G R A H E A X B R O O P A O F
R N S F T F H P P D W S I Z C N P L B F
Y W I J E C J S D A W D S T E W U L E D
W K Z C S Q K T C V R R M E L Y W T V M
E N U H O Y I V Y I S A K S E E D S S C
A T O G L L D M C D S C C F Z Y F I V M
T X L T C M E W N C H U J H P B R N L J
H Q E L E P D E O K N L W C E T E N Y N
E B G C C S I T V H M A O M A L E E S X
R B N T Y R N P H B H S X D N C M T L N
X H A X F H T E J Z S E N S H S A B P Z
K K B H H P Y L C A Z I F W Z F N C L B
N C V B Z R Y D C K L T P F L V J L Q X
H L B G A B D I F E L Y R T E W J O P K
Q S L R R O P K M S V A F R Q R Q W R H
R S B N S N C N J K K F C E V X T N O J
B I K E C E W L H E A T H E R D W S M F
L M Q M N S B U N N Y D N A M O D E L C
```

ANDY	DRACULA	LAB	NICOLE
ANGELOU	EFFERTS	LIBRARY	NOTES
ART	FREEMAN	LIPS	PICASSO
BIKE	FRIENDS	MARTHAS	PROM
BONES	FROG	MASCOT	RACHEL
BUNNY	GLASS	MELINDA	SEEDS
CLOSET	GLOBE	MERRYWEATHER	SPEAK
CLOWNS	HEATHER	MISS	STALL
COPS	IT	MODEL	TAXI
DAVID	IVY	NECK	TENNIS
DONUTS	KEEN	NECKLACE	TREE

Speak Word Search 1 Answer Key

```
M A R T H A S    G T I K L I P S    S G
E           O    R   A   A   D   P T L
R         T F    A   P   X   O   O A O
R       N E      S   S   S   C   N L B
Y      I C       L       R   E     L E
W      N O       I V Y I S     S E E T S
E      U L       E     N C       F I
A      O T       S     E         R N
T      L C       I     T         E N
H      E E       R               E E
E        S       N               M T
R                Y               A
                                 N   C
         R       C                   L
       A B O P K M                   O P
   S S   B N C     H E A T H E R     W R
   B I K E E N S B U N N Y D N A M O D E L
```

ANDY	DRACULA	LAB	NICOLE
ANGELOU	EFFERTS	LIBRARY	NOTES
ART	FREEMAN	LIPS	PICASSO
BIKE	FRIENDS	MARTHAS	PROM
BONES	FROG	MASCOT	RACHEL
BUNNY	GLASS	MELINDA	SEEDS
CLOSET	GLOBE	MERRYWEATHER	SPEAK
CLOWNS	HEATHER	MISS	STALL
COPS	IT	MODEL	TAXI
DAVID	IVY	NECK	TENNIS
DONUTS	KEEN	NECKLACE	TREE

Copyrighted

Speak Word Search 2

```
B L N S Z M J E J R K T S T C P F T L K
S N A R P H A E X N S E E E G L R O I K
G L O B E E X R I F R I E N D S O C P Q
J F Q J V A A T T T V F D N O R G S S W
M H Z G B T M K W H F J S I N T H A E D
G O R Y N H B E K E A C A S U L E M F T
W Z D N P E X H R B V S R E T I P S S Q
R N T E Y R C T Y R Y T T T S B R E R L
A M A Y L P S K K C Y F Z T C R O L I V
D M X N P T W H Q L F W L E J A M O V V
N P I C A S S O C O P S E G Y R B C Y C
I E X S R J T Q B W A S H A V Y H I Y S
L C C S S B A T W N L A C R T M J N K P
E X F K O Z L Q T S U L A F B H N B W E
M X R N L V L D Z O C G R F K U E F K Y
K Y E Y W A I W L V A Z S U B G C R Z C
P S E P Q V C E F X R G S S K D K K K X
V L M J A G G E W W D D S D P N B Q W Y
W Y A D Y N C H X L R D R M H X K C G K
C Q N Q A H J X G F S D D T F Q B T Y Y
```

ANDY	EFFERTS	LIPS	PROM
ANGELOU	FREEMAN	MARTHAS	RACHEL
ART	FRIENDS	MASCOT	SEEDS
BIKE	FROG	MELINDA	SPEAK
BONES	GLASS	MERRYWEATHER	STALL
BUNNY	GLOBE	MISS	SUFFRAGETTES
CLOSET	HEATHER	MODEL	TAXI
CLOWNS	IT	NECK	TENNIS
COPS	IVY	NECKLACE	TREE
DAVID	KEEN	NICOLE	
DONUTS	LAB	NOTES	
DRACULA	LIBRARY	PICASSO	

Speak Word Search 2 Answer Key

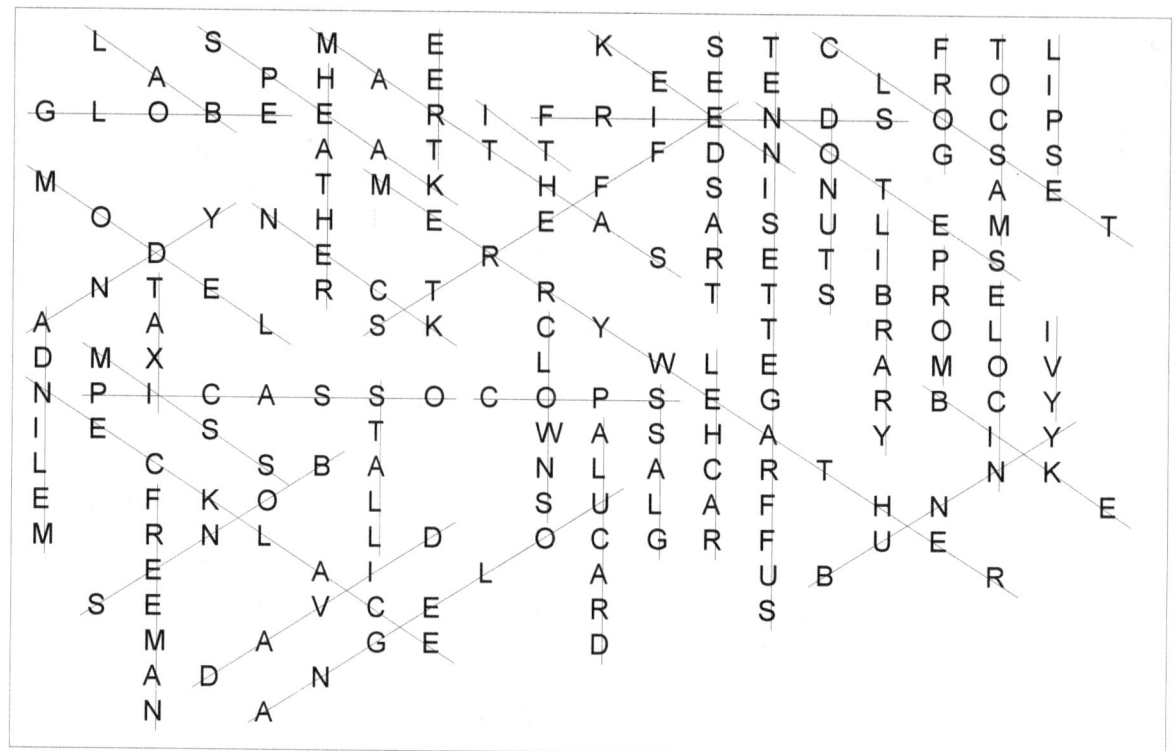

ANDY	EFFERTS	LIPS	PROM
ANGELOU	FREEMAN	MARTHAS	RACHEL
ART	FRIENDS	MASCOT	SEEDS
BIKE	FROG	MELINDA	SPEAK
BONES	GLASS	MERRYWEATHER	STALL
BUNNY	GLOBE	MISS	SUFFRAGETTES
CLOSET	HEATHER	MODEL	TAXI
CLOWNS	IT	NECK	TENNIS
COPS	IVY	NECKLACE	TREE
DAVID	KEEN	NICOLE	
DONUTS	LAB	NOTES	
DRACULA	LIBRARY	PICASSO	

Speak Word Search 3

```
P I C A S S O B I K E B R A C H E L
B S Q D A T F X Y B L U D V M P F C
L J E D H J A G G H S N C D O M F V
P E L P T F W L X X I N S G D N E F
S S I M R S R A L L N Y W B E G R L
M T P X A W L I E T N L A E L L T Q
A W S N M U R M E H N L R O N A S W
S C B P C P G K M N T T B F E S W P
C Z L A W H D E N V D E T I C S D W
O Y R O F G U E X O P S X J K M T R
T D D P S O D N Q Y T A L R N R E W
G R M B L E R Y R B T E T T C L J V
D Z D E I F T E F W S S S H O K V S
I G G J B V H W C B K T G C P J N H
V N N Q R T W Y Z A O U I C R W N M
A R T T A F R E E M A N F R O G J Y
D T X E R F R P K H C O E L M P V Y
I X H K Y P S A N D Y D C S W I S G
```

- Animal Melinda compared herself to when she was near Andy (5)
- Artist who inspired Melinda (7)
- Biology teacher who created interesting assignments (4)
- Book Melinda read on Halloween (7)
- David was Melinda's ___ partner in Biology class. (3)
- Event at which Rachel broke up with Andy (4)
- Exclusive group of girls who performed good deeds (7)
- He invited Melinda to a party after a basketball game. (5)
- Heather told Melinda they could no longer be this. (7)
- Her books were banned in the library; her poster picture was in Melinda's closet (7)
- Inspiration for Ivy's art project (6)
- Kind of supplies Melinda's parents gave her for Christmas (3)
- Major symbol in the book; subject of Melinda's art project (4)
- Melinda almost beat Nicole at this sport (6)
- Melinda asked her dad to buy these for her. (5)
- Melinda did not do this very much. (5)
- Melinda held this up to Andy's throat when he tried to rape her again (5)
- Melinda tried to warn her about Andy. (6)
- Melinda warned others about him. (4)
- Melinda wrote a warning about Andy on the bathroom ___ door. (5)
- Melinda's dad's transportation to the airport (4)
- Melinda's transportation to the place where she was raped (4)
- Method of communication for Melinda's family (5)
- Mr. Freeman used this to assign art projects at the beginning of the year. (5)
- Nickname Melinda had for Andy (2)
- Only teacher Melinda talked to (7)
- Part-time job for Heather (5)
- People Melinda called after being raped (4)
- Place where Melinda confided in Rachel about being raped (7)
- Place where Melinda got stuck for skipping class (4)
- Place where Melinda hides at school (6)
- She found Melinda after Andy tried to rape her a second time. (6)
- She found her voice in the end. (7)
- She gave Melinda a card on Valentine's Day. (7)
- She helped Melinda draw a more realistic tree. (3)
- Store where Melinda's mother worked (7)
- Subject of dissection in Biology (4)
- Teacher who was xenophobic, bigoted, and unjust (4)
- The school ___ kept changing (6)
- They were scabbed over from being chewed on (4)
- Turkey ___ were part of Melinda's art project (5)
- What Melinda's dad bought on Thanksgiving (6)

Speak Word Search 3 Answer Key

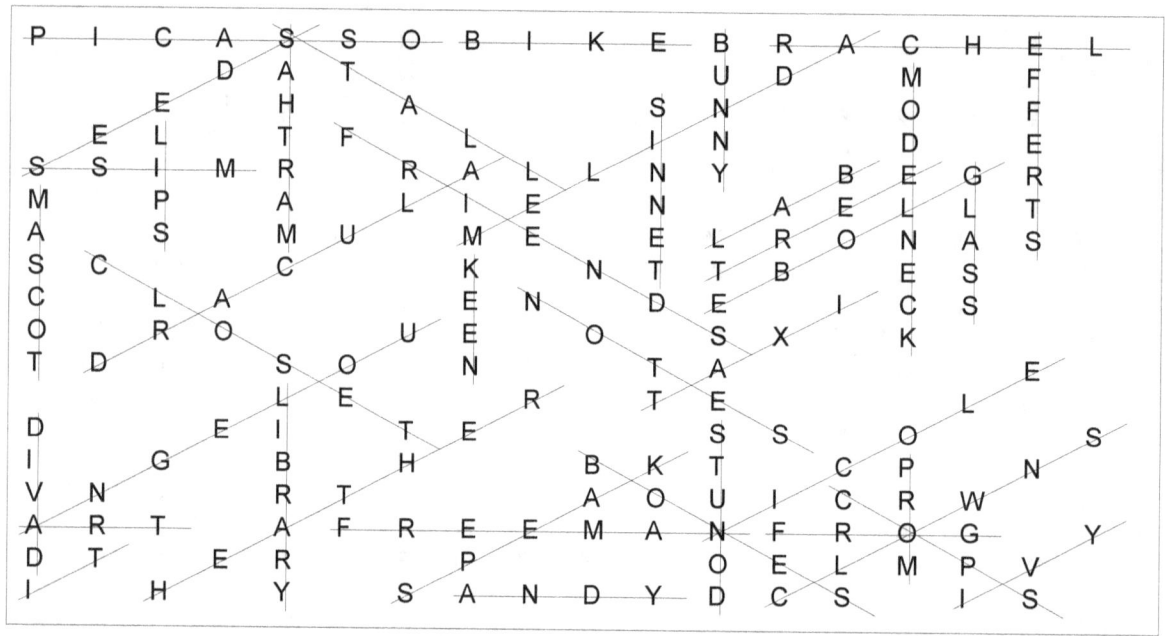

Animal Melinda compared herself to when she was near Andy (5)
Artist who inspired Melinda (7)
Biology teacher who created interesting assignments (4)
Book Melinda read on Halloween (7)
David was Melinda's ___ partner in Biology class. (3)
Event at which Rachel broke up with Andy (4)
Exclusive group of girls who performed good deeds (7)
He invited Melinda to a party after a basketball game. (5)
Heather told Melinda they could no longer be this. (7)
Her books were banned in the library; her poster picture was in Melinda's closet (7)
Inspiration for Ivy's art project (6)
Kind of supplies Melinda's parents gave her for Christmas (3)
Major symbol in the book; subject of Melinda's art project (4)
Melinda almost beat Nicole at this sport (6)
Melinda asked her dad to buy these for her. (5)
Melinda did not do this very much. (5)
Melinda held this up to Andy's throat when he tried to rape her again (5)
Melinda tried to warn her about Andy. (6)
Melinda warned others about him. (4)
Melinda wrote a warning about Andy on the bathroom ___ door. (5)
Melinda's dad's transportation to the airport (4)
Melinda's transportation to the place where she was raped (4)
Method of communication for Melinda's family (5)
Mr. Freeman used this to assign art projects at the beginning of the year. (5)
Nickname Melinda had for Andy (2)
Only teacher Melinda talked to (7)
Part-time job for Heather (5)
People Melinda called after being raped (4)
Place where Melinda confided in Rachel about being raped (7)
Place where Melinda got stuck for skipping class (4)
Place where Melinda hides at school (6)
She found Melinda after Andy tried to rape her a second time. (6)
She found her voice in the end. (7)
She gave Melinda a card on Valentine's Day. (7)
She helped Melinda draw a more realistic tree. (3)
Store where Melinda's mother worked (7)
Subject of dissection in Biology (4)
Teacher who was xenophobic, bigoted, and unjust (4)
The school ___ kept changing (6)
They were scabbed over from being chewed on (4)
Turkey ___ were part of Melinda's art project (5)
What Melinda's dad bought on Thanksgiving (6)

Speak Word Search 4

```
A N E H N E C K L A C E P I V Y H P
N C F Q E R K T B T K X I R Q X X B
G T F J X A S B J A N R C H O K X Q
E R E B T V T D F X F H A W N M Q G
L Q R G Z Q U H R I J Z S R Y E Q D
O H T N Q R N J E A S R S L G L H M
U L S Q I J O B G R C L O I M I M W
L I N M Y C D G O M T U N B Q N A R
H P I M D Z O H V N R T L R D D R G
Q S C S N W O L C L E H C A R A T H
S W C E A Q L R E N E S V R G I H P
P Y C C T A X Z N A P I S Y K S A V
G K F W T R A I C M D B P G M E S K
L N R S N T S L O E F U E L A E E K
O X O F V J O D P E V N A A S D L N
B C G T F S E L S R N N K S C S A T
E B I K E L W S C F Y Y K S O S B H
F T T T B S U F F R A G E T T E S K
```

- Animal Melinda compared herself to when she was near Andy (5)
- Artist who inspired Melinda (7)
- Biology teacher who created interesting assignments (4)
- Book Melinda read on Halloween (7)
- David was Melinda's ___ partner in Biology class. (3)
- Event at which Rachel broke up with Andy (4)
- Exclusive group of girls who performed good deeds (7)
- He invited Melinda to a party after a basketball game. (5)
- Heather's Christmas present from Melinda (8)
- Her books were banned in the library; her poster picture was in Melinda's closet (7)
- Inspiration for Ivy's art project (6)
- Kind of supplies Melinda's parents gave her for Christmas (3)
- Major symbol in the book; subject of Melinda's art project (4)
- Melinda almost beat Nicole at this sport (6)
- Melinda asked her dad to buy these for her. (5)
- Melinda did not do this very much. (5)
- Melinda held this up to Andy's throat when he tried to rape her again (5)
- Melinda tried to warn her about Andy. (6)
- Melinda warned others about him. (4)
- Melinda wrote a warning about Andy on the bathroom ___ door. (5)
- Melinda's dad's transportation to the airport (4)
- Melinda's transportation to the place where she was raped (4)
- Method of communication for Melinda's family (5)
- Mr. Freeman used this to assign art projects at the beginning of the year. (5)
- Nickname Melinda had for Andy (2)
- Only teacher Melinda talked to (7)
- Part-time job for Heather (5)
- People Melinda called after being raped (4)
- Place where Melinda confided in Rachel about being raped (7)
- Place where Melinda got stuck for skipping class (4)
- Place where Melinda hides at school (6)
- She found Melinda after Andy tried to rape her a second time. (6)
- She found her voice in the end. (7)
- She gave Melinda a card on Valentine's Day. (7)
- She helped Melinda draw a more realistic tree. (3)
- Store where Melinda's mother worked (7)
- Subject of dissection in Biology (4)
- Teacher who was xenophobic, bigoted, and unjust (4)
- The school ___ kept changing (6)
- They were scabbed over from being chewed on (4)
- Turkey ___ were part of Melinda's art project (5)
- What Melinda's dad bought on Thanksgiving (6)
- Women Melinda did a report about (12)

Speak Word Search 4 Answer Key

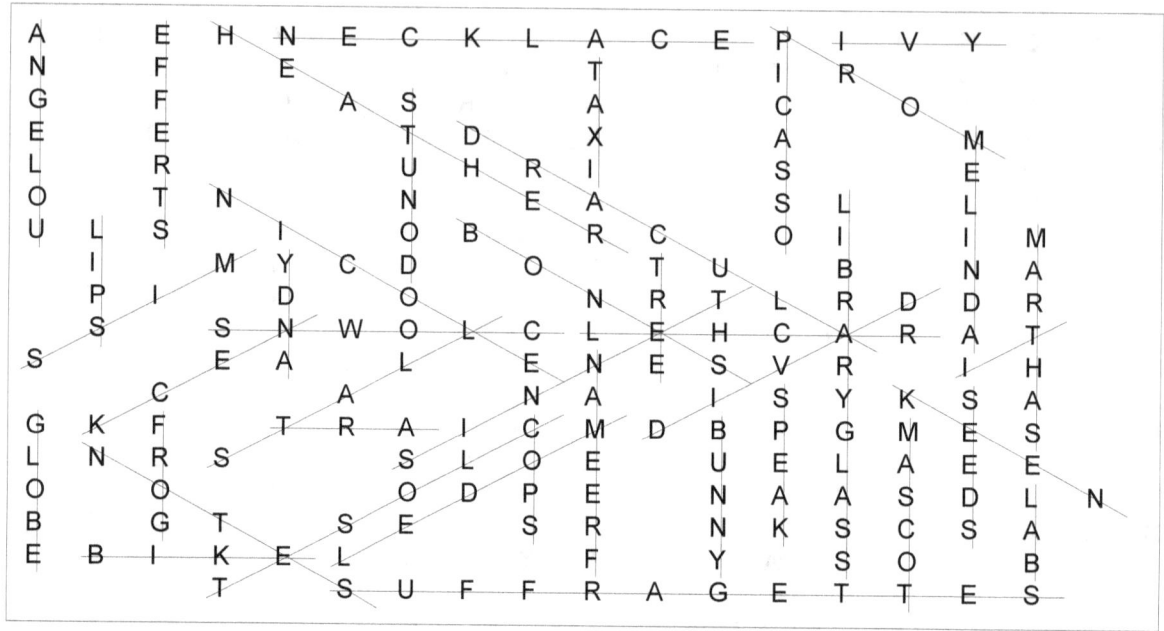

Animal Melinda compared herself to when she was near Andy (5)
Artist who inspired Melinda (7)
Biology teacher who created interesting assignments (4)
Book Melinda read on Halloween (7)
David was Melinda's ___ partner in Biology class. (3)
Event at which Rachel broke up with Andy (4)
Exclusive group of girls who performed good deeds (7)
He invited Melinda to a party after a basketball game. (5)
Heather's Christmas present from Melinda (8)
Her books were banned in the library; her poster picture was in Melinda's closet (7)
Inspiration for Ivy's art project (6)
Kind of supplies Melinda's parents gave her for Christmas (3)
Major symbol in the book; subject of Melinda's art project (4)
Melinda almost beat Nicole at this sport (6)
Melinda asked her dad to buy these for her. (5)
Melinda did not do this very much. (5)
Melinda held this up to Andy's throat when he tried to rape her again (5)
Melinda tried to warn her about Andy. (6)
Melinda warned others about him. (4)
Melinda wrote a warning about Andy on the bathroom ___ door. (5)

Melinda's dad's transportation to the airport (4)
Melinda's transportation to the place where she was raped (4)
Method of communication for Melinda's family (5)
Mr. Freeman used this to assign art projects at the beginning of the year. (5)
Nickname Melinda had for Andy (2)
Only teacher Melinda talked to (7)
Part-time job for Heather (5)
People Melinda called after being raped (4)
Place where Melinda confided in Rachel about being raped (7)
Place where Melinda got stuck for skipping class (4)
Place where Melinda hides at school (6)
She found Melinda after Andy tried to rape her a second time. (6)
She found her voice in the end. (7)
She gave Melinda a card on Valentine's Day. (7)
She helped Melinda draw a more realistic tree. (3)
Store where Melinda's mother worked (7)
Subject of dissection in Biology (4)
Teacher who was xenophobic, bigoted, and unjust (4)
The school ___ kept changing (6)
They were scabbed over from being chewed on (4)
Turkey ___ were part of Melinda's art project (5)
What Melinda's dad bought on Thanksgiving (6)
Women Melinda did a report about (12)

Speak Crossword 1

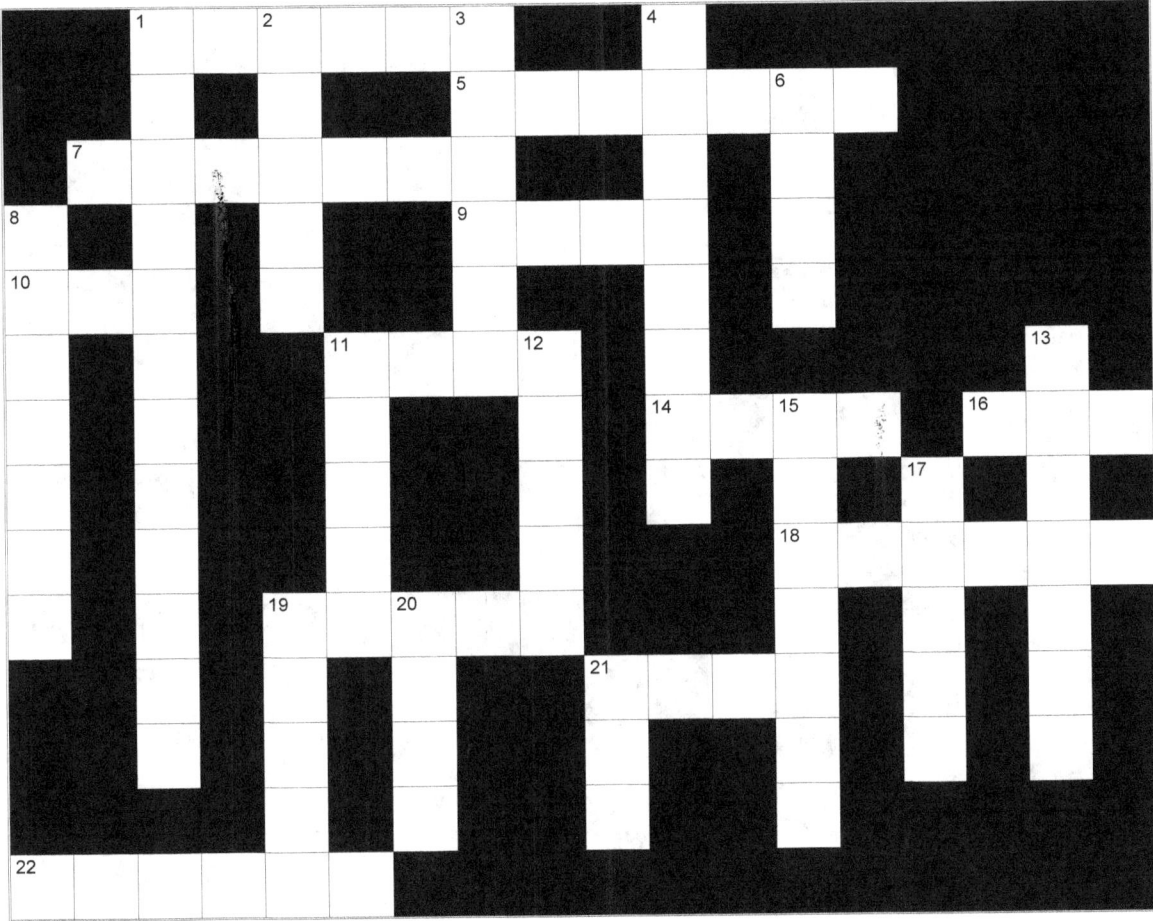

Across
1. The school ___ kept changing
5. Store where Melinda's mother worked
7. Only teacher Melinda talked to
9. Teacher who was xenophobic, bigoted, and unjust
10. She helped Melinda draw a more realistic tree.
11. Place where Melinda got stuck for skipping class
14. People Melinda called after being raped
16. Kind of supplies Melinda's parents gave her for Christmas
18. Place where Melinda hides at school
19. Melinda held this up to Andy's throat when he tried to rape her again
21. They were scabbed over from being chewed on
22. Melinda tried to warn her about Andy.

Down
1. Name of the school
2. Melinda did not do this very much.
3. Melinda almost beat Nicole at this sport
4. Heather's Christmas present from Melinda
6. Major symbol in the book; subject of Melinda's art project
8. Place where Melinda confided in Rachel about being raped
11. Part-time job for Heather
12. Melinda asked her dad to buy these for her.
13. Heather told Melinda they could no longer be this.
15. Artist who inspired Melinda
17. Turkey ___ were part of Melinda's art project
19. Mr. Freeman used this to assign art projects at the beginning of the year.
20. Melinda warned others about him.
21. David was Melinda's ___ partner in Biology class.

Speak Crossword 1 Answer Key

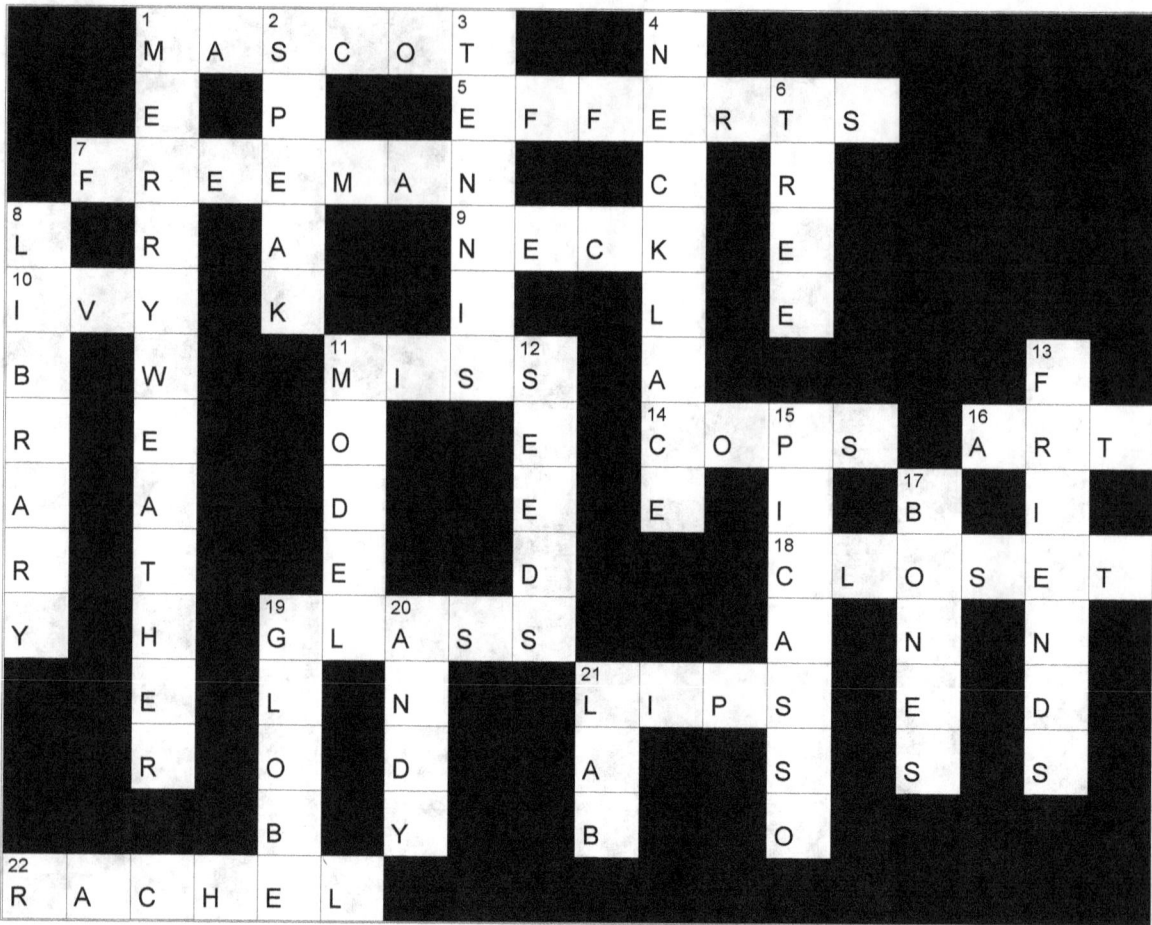

Across
1. The school ___ kept changing
5. Store where Melinda's mother worked
7. Only teacher Melinda talked to
9. Teacher who was xenophobic, bigoted, and unjust
10. She helped Melinda draw a more realistic tree.
11. Place where Melinda got stuck for skipping class
14. People Melinda called after being raped
16. Kind of supplies Melinda's parents gave her for Christmas
18. Place where Melinda hides at school
19. Melinda held this up to Andy's throat when he tried to rape her again
21. They were scabbed over from being chewed on
22. Melinda tried to warn her about Andy.

Down
1. Name of the school
2. Melinda did not do this very much.
3. Melinda almost beat Nicole at this sport
4. Heather's Christmas present from Melinda
6. Major symbol in the book; subject of Melinda's art project
8. Place where Melinda confided in Rachel about being raped
11. Part-time job for Heather
12. Melinda asked her dad to buy these for her.
13. Heather told Melinda they could no longer be this.
15. Artist who inspired Melinda
17. Turkey ___ were part of Melinda's art project
19. Mr. Freeman used this to assign art projects at the beginning of the year.
20. Melinda warned others about him.
21. David was Melinda's ___ partner in Biology class.

Speak Crossword 2

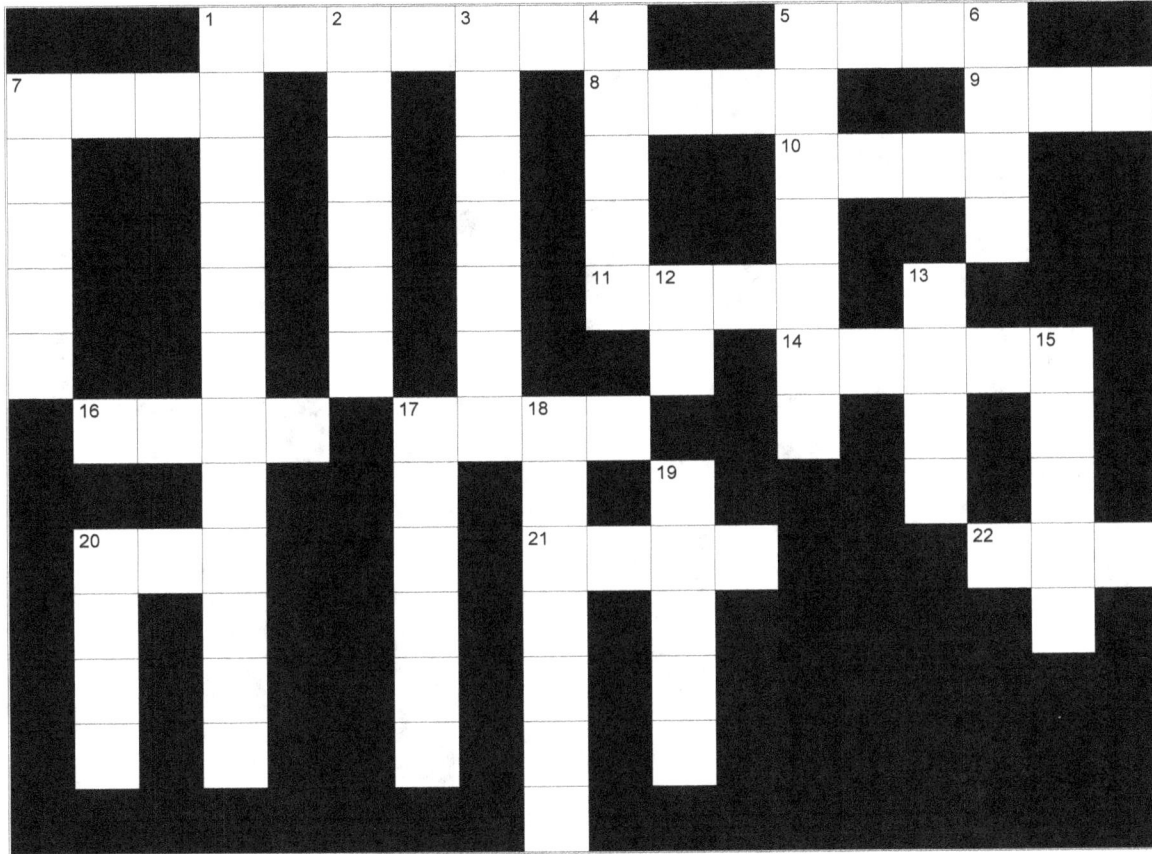

Across
1. Exclusive group of girls who performed good deeds
5. Event at which Rachel broke up with Andy
7. Melinda's transportation to the place where she was raped
8. Melinda's dad's transportation to the airport
9. She helped Melinda draw a more realistic tree.
10. People Melinda called after being raped
11. They were scabbed over from being chewed on
14. Melinda asked her dad to buy these for her.
16. Biology teacher who created interesting assignments
17. Major symbol in the book; subject of Melinda's art project
20. Kind of supplies Melinda's parents gave her for Christmas
21. Subject of dissection in Biology
22. David was Melinda's ___ partner in Biology class.

Down
1. Name of the school
2. Melinda tried to warn her about Andy.
3. She gave Melinda a card on Valentine's Day.
4. Melinda wrote a warning about Andy on the bathroom ___ door.
5. Artist who inspired Melinda
6. Place where Melinda got stuck for skipping class
7. Animal Melinda compared herself to when she was near Andy
12. Nickname Melinda had for Andy
13. Teacher who was xenophobic, bigoted, and unjust
15. Melinda did not do this very much.
17. Melinda almost beat Nicole at this sport
18. Store where Melinda's mother worked
19. Method of communication for Melinda's family
20. Melinda warned others about him.

Speak Crossword 2 Answer Key

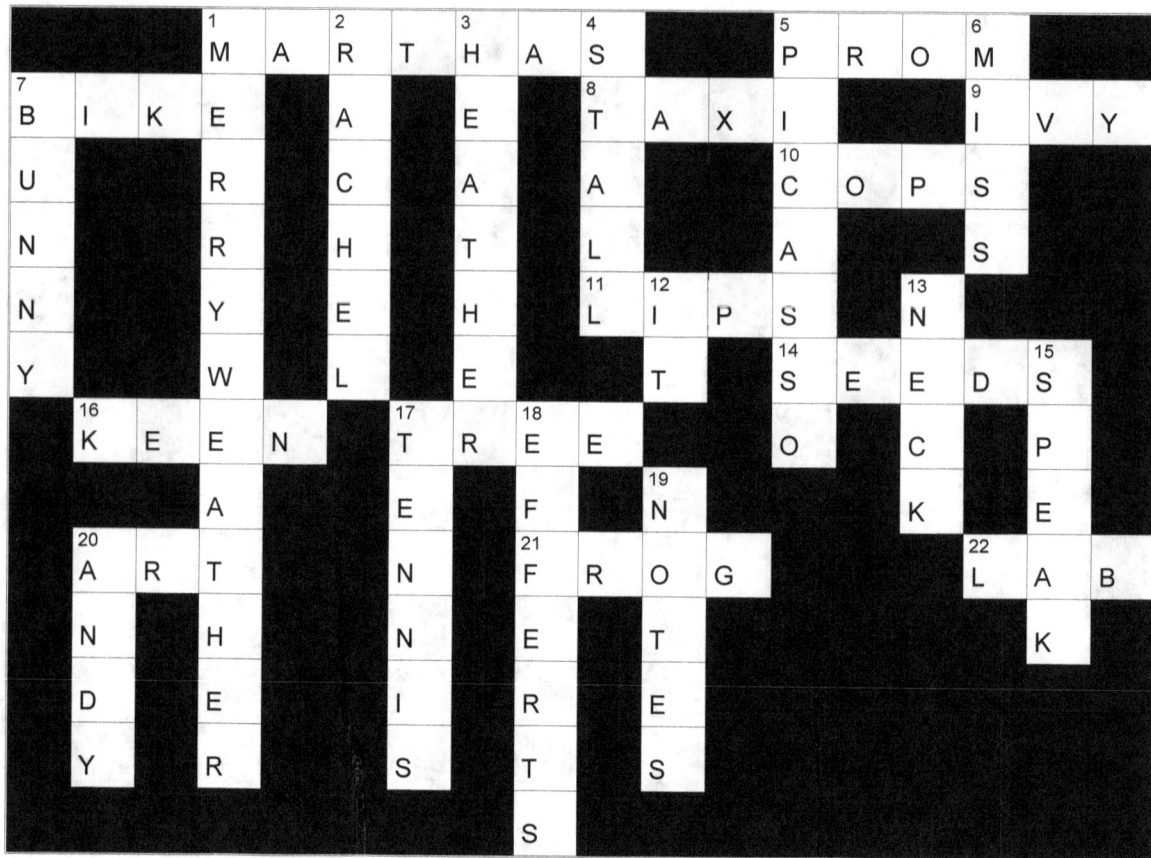

Across
1. Exclusive group of girls who performed good deeds
5. Event at which Rachel broke up with Andy
7. Melinda's transportation to the place where she was raped
8. Melinda's dad's transportation to the airport
9. She helped Melinda draw a more realistic tree.
10. People Melinda called after being raped
11. They were scabbed over from being chewed on
14. Melinda asked her dad to buy these for her.
16. Biology teacher who created interesting assignments
17. Major symbol in the book; subject of Melinda's art project
20. Kind of supplies Melinda's parents gave her for Christmas
21. Subject of dissection in Biology
22. David was Melinda's ___ partner in Biology class.

Down
1. Name of the school
2. Melinda tried to warn her about Andy.
3. She gave Melinda a card on Valentine's Day.
4. Melinda wrote a warning about Andy on the bathroom ___ door.
5. Artist who inspired Melinda
6. Place where Melinda got stuck for skipping class
7. Animal Melinda compared herself to when she was near Andy
12. Nickname Melinda had for Andy
13. Teacher who was xenophobic, bigoted, and unjust
15. Melinda did not do this very much.
17. Melinda almost beat Nicole at this sport
18. Store where Melinda's mother worked
19. Method of communication for Melinda's family
20. Melinda warned others about him.

Speak Crossword 3

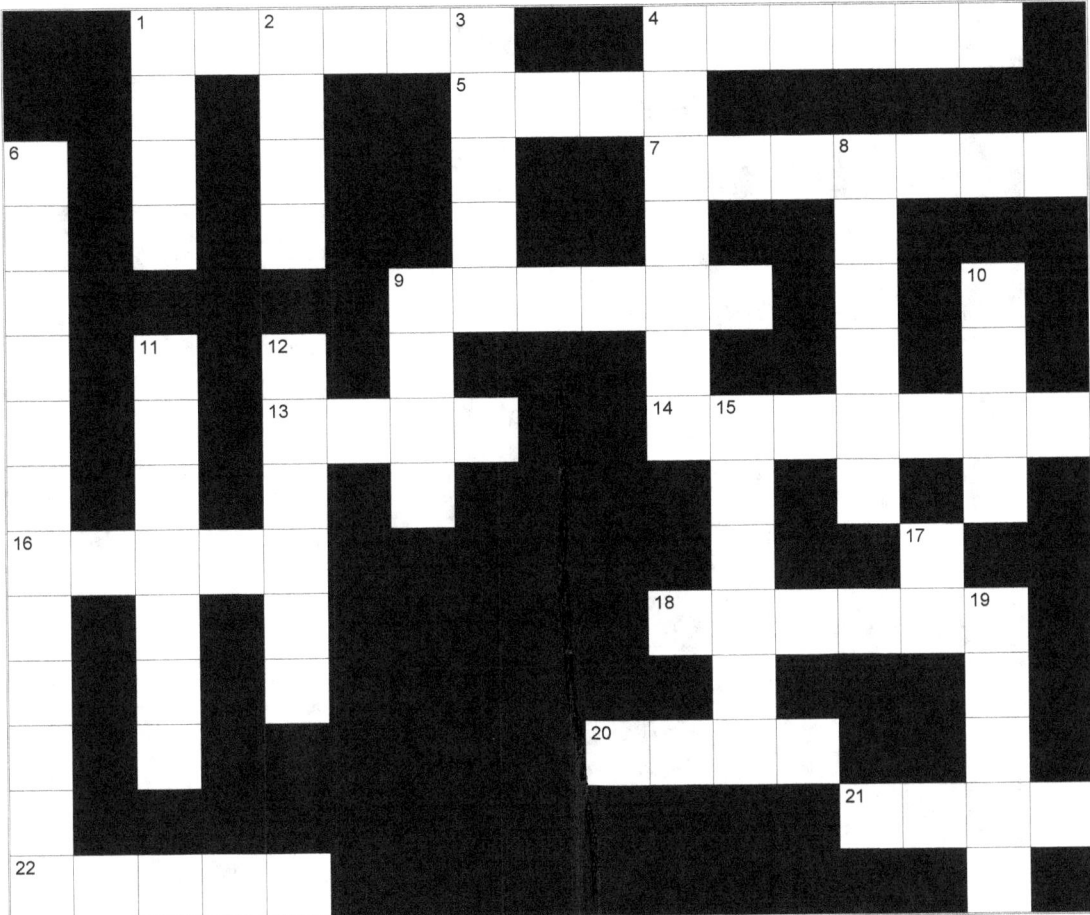

Across
1. Melinda almost beat Nicole at this sport
4. The school ___ kept changing
5. Major symbol in the book; subject of Melinda's art project
7. Place where Melinda confided in Rachel about being raped
9. Inspiration for Ivy's art project
13. They were scabbed over from being chewed on
14. Her books were banned in the library; her poster picture was in Melinda's closet
16. Melinda held this up to Andy's throat when he tried to rape her again
18. What Melinda's dad bought on Thanksgiving
20. Biology teacher who created interesting assignments
21. Melinda warned others about him.
22. Melinda did not do this very much.

Down
1. Melinda's dad's transportation to the airport
2. Teacher who was xenophobic, bigoted, and unjust
3. Melinda wrote a warning about Andy on the bathroom ___ door.
4. She found her voice in the end.
6. Women Melinda did a report about
8. Melinda tried to warn her about Andy.
9. People Melinda called after being raped
10. Subject of dissection in Biology
11. Artist who inspired Melinda
12. Place where Melinda hides at school
15. She found Melinda after Andy tried to rape her a second time.
17. Nickname Melinda had for Andy
19. Melinda asked her dad to buy these for her.

Speak Crossword 3 Answer Key

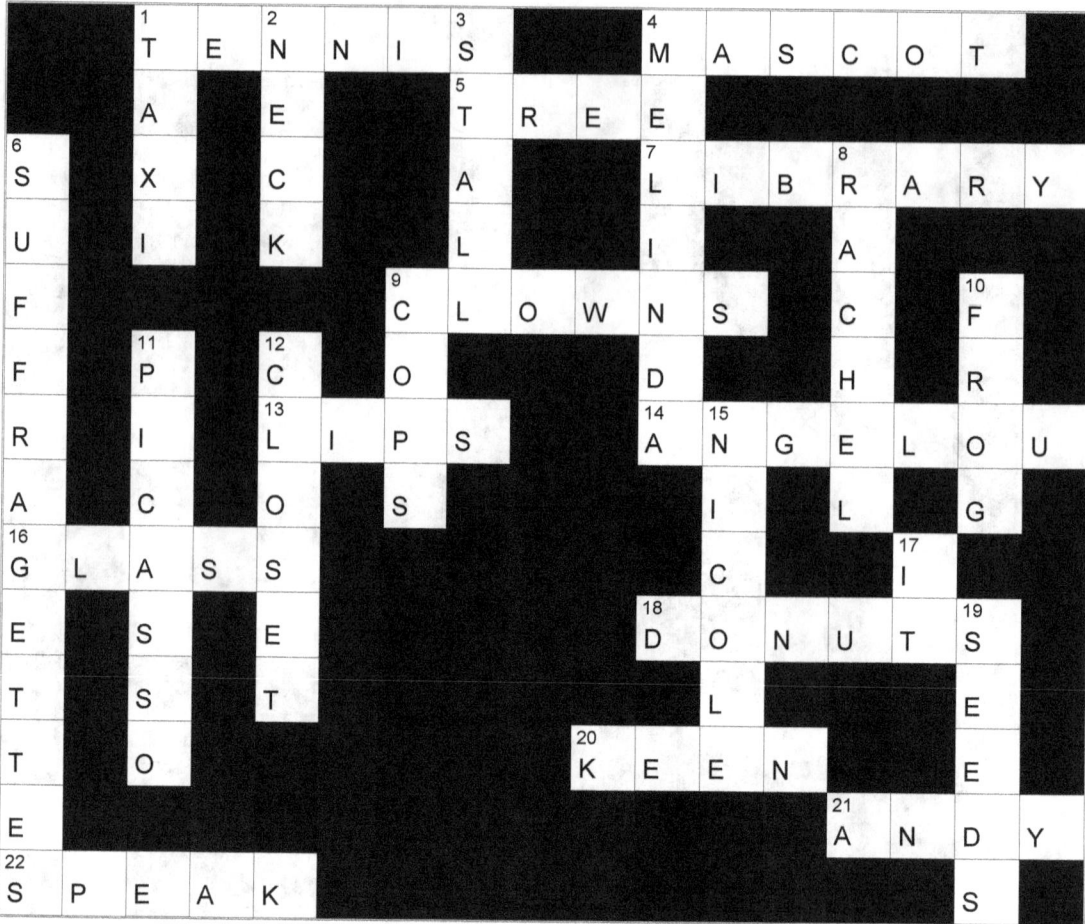

Across
1. Melinda almost beat Nicole at this sport
4. The school ___ kept changing
5. Major symbol in the book; subject of Melinda's art project
7. Place where Melinda confided in Rachel about being raped
9. Inspiration for Ivy's art project
13. They were scabbed over from being chewed on
14. Her books were banned in the library; her poster picture was in Melinda's closet
16. Melinda held this up to Andy's throat when he tried to rape her again
18. What Melinda's dad bought on Thanksgiving
20. Biology teacher who created interesting assignments
21. Melinda warned others about him.
22. Melinda did not do this very much.

Down
1. Melinda's dad's transportation to the airport
2. Teacher who was xenophobic, bigoted, and unjust
3. Melinda wrote a warning about Andy on the bathroom ___ door.
4. She found her voice in the end.
6. Women Melinda did a report about
8. Melinda tried to warn her about Andy.
9. People Melinda called after being raped
10. Subject of dissection in Biology
11. Artist who inspired Melinda
12. Place where Melinda hides at school
15. She found Melinda after Andy tried to rape her a second time.
17. Nickname Melinda had for Andy
19. Melinda asked her dad to buy these for her.

Speak Crossword 4

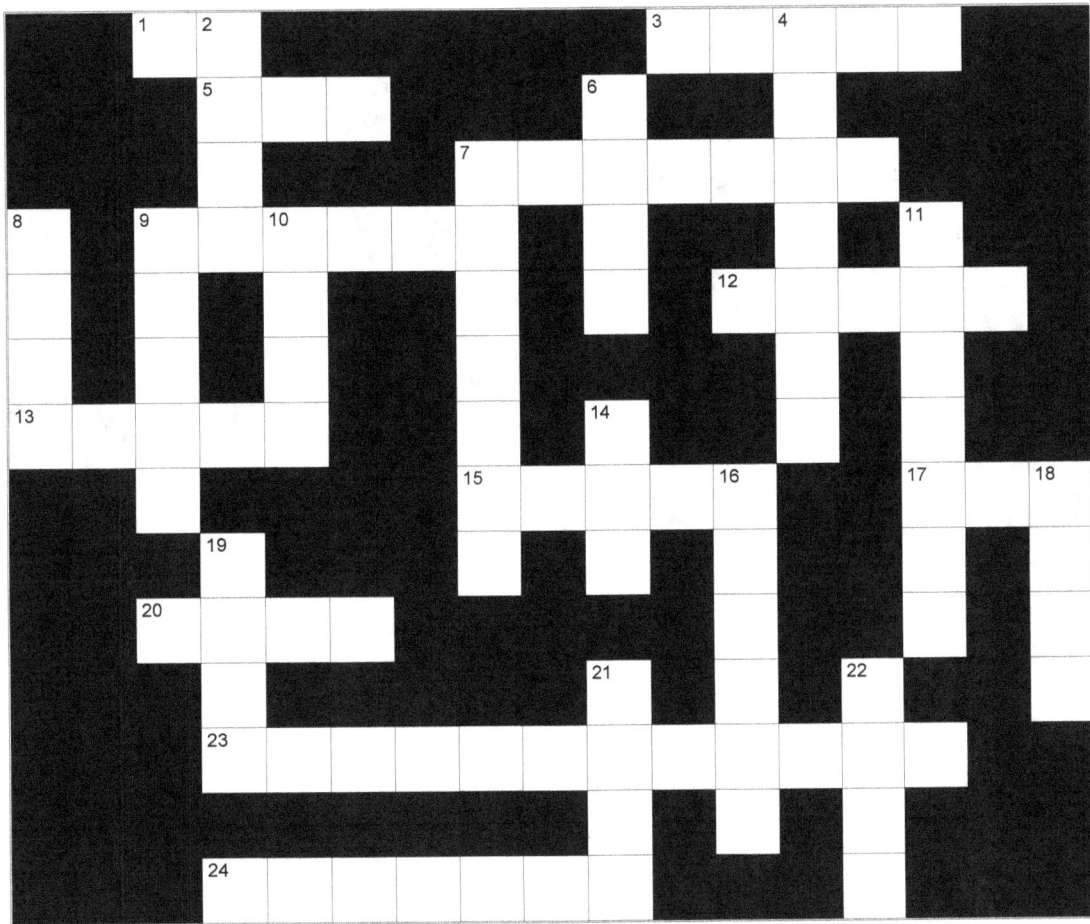

Across
1. Nickname Melinda had for Andy
3. Part-time job for Heather
5. Kind of supplies Melinda's parents gave her for Christmas
7. Exclusive group of girls who performed good deeds
9. She found Melinda after Andy tried to rape her a second time.
12. Animal Melinda compared herself to when she was near Andy
13. Melinda asked her dad to buy these for her.
15. He invited Melinda to a party after a basketball game.
17. David was Melinda's ___ partner in Biology class.
20. Major symbol in the book; subject of Melinda's art project
23. Name of the school
24. Only teacher Melinda talked to

Down
2. Melinda's dad's transportation to the airport
4. Book Melinda read on Halloween
6. Subject of dissection in Biology
7. She found her voice in the end.
8. Place where Melinda got stuck for skipping class
9. Method of communication for Melinda's family
10. People Melinda called after being raped
11. Her books were banned in the library; her poster picture was in Melinda's closet
14. She helped Melinda draw a more realistic tree.
16. What Melinda's dad bought on Thanksgiving
18. Melinda's transportation to the place where she was raped
19. Event at which Rachel broke up with Andy
21. Biology teacher who created interesting assignments
22. Teacher who was xenophobic, bigoted, and unjust

Speak Crossword 4 Answer Key

Across
1. Nickname Melinda had for Andy
3. Part-time job for Heather
5. Kind of supplies Melinda's parents gave her for Christmas
7. Exclusive group of girls who performed good deeds
9. She found Melinda after Andy tried to rape her a second time.
12. Animal Melinda compared herself to when she was near Andy
13. Melinda asked her dad to buy these for her.
15. He invited Melinda to a party after a basketball game.
17. David was Melinda's ___ partner in Biology class.
20. Major symbol in the book; subject of Melinda's art project
23. Name of the school
24. Only teacher Melinda talked to

Down
2. Melinda's dad's transportation to the airport
4. Book Melinda read on Halloween
6. Subject of dissection in Biology
7. She found her voice in the end.
8. Place where Melinda got stuck for skipping class
9. Method of communication for Melinda's family
10. People Melinda called after being raped
11. Her books were banned in the library; her poster picture was in Melinda's closet
14. She helped Melinda draw a more realistic tree.
16. What Melinda's dad bought on Thanksgiving
18. Melinda's transportation to the place where she was raped
19. Event at which Rachel broke up with Andy
21. Biology teacher who created interesting assignments
22. Teacher who was xenophobic, bigoted, and unjust

Speak

DRACULA	LAB	NECKLACE	TREE	LIPS
MARTHAS	DAVID	COPS	GLASS	HEATHER
MODEL	TAXI	FREE SPACE	KEEN	MASCOT
LIBRARY	PROM	ANDY	NICOLE	CLOSET
GLOBE	DONUTS	FROG	ANGELOU	BONES

Speak

FRIENDS	BIKE	EFFERTS	CLOWNS	IVY
NECK	FREEMAN	TENNIS	IT	STALL
SUFFRAGETTES	NOTES	FREE SPACE	PICASSO	MERRYWEATHER
SPEAK	MISS	MELINDA	ART	RACHEL
BONES	ANGELOU	FROG	DONUTS	GLOBE

Speak

LIPS	ANGELOU	MASCOT	RACHEL	HEATHER
DAVID	MELINDA	MARTHAS	PICASSO	SPEAK
TAXI	LAB	FREE SPACE	MODEL	NECK
MERRYWEATHER	FROG	ART	BONES	FREEMAN
PROM	MISS	IT	ANDY	CLOSET

Speak

GLASS	TREE	DONUTS	SEEDS	NOTES
SUFFRAGETTES	COPS	FRIENDS	NECKLACE	STALL
LIBRARY	NICOLE	FREE SPACE	EFFERTS	GLOBE
BIKE	BUNNY	KEEN	IVY	TENNIS
CLOSET	ANDY	IT	MISS	PROM

Speak

MASCOT	IT	LAB	CLOSET	ANGELOU
MODEL	LIBRARY	NECK	FRIENDS	DONUTS
MELINDA	MISS	FREE SPACE	GLOBE	FREEMAN
HEATHER	IVY	STALL	EFFERTS	TAXI
PROM	NOTES	NECKLACE	MARTHAS	FROG

Speak

TREE	BONES	TENNIS	CLOWNS	ART
BIKE	SPEAK	LIPS	PICASSO	GLASS
RACHEL	SEEDS	FREE SPACE	NICOLE	ANDY
KEEN	DRACULA	DAVID	BUNNY	COPS
FROG	MARTHAS	NECKLACE	NOTES	PROM

Speak

MODEL	MELINDA	CLOSET	NECKLACE	BONES
SPEAK	COPS	FRIENDS	BUNNY	MARTHAS
LAB	KEEN	FREE SPACE	FREEMAN	PROM
ART	NOTES	MASCOT	GLOBE	MISS
SEEDS	IT	DAVID	PICASSO	ANDY

Speak

GLASS	CLOWNS	LIBRARY	IVY	TAXI
LIPS	NECK	DRACULA	HEATHER	NICOLE
TENNIS	MERRYWEATHER	FREE SPACE	FROG	EFFERTS
ANGELOU	STALL	SUFFRAGETTES	DONUTS	TREE
ANDY	PICASSO	DAVID	IT	SEEDS

Speak

BUNNY	ANGELOU	LIPS	IT	CLOSET
PICASSO	BIKE	LAB	TENNIS	BONES
PROM	STALL	FREE SPACE	LIBRARY	RACHEL
MARTHAS	HEATHER	MASCOT	GLASS	TAXI
DRACULA	MELINDA	ANDY	SPEAK	CLOWNS

Speak

GLOBE	NECKLACE	COPS	NOTES	KEEN
IVY	TREE	ART	SEEDS	EFFERTS
NICOLE	MISS	FREE SPACE	MERRYWEATHER	FREEMAN
DONUTS	FRIENDS	NECK	FROG	SUFFRAGETTES
CLOWNS	SPEAK	ANDY	MELINDA	DRACULA

Speak

FROG	NICOLE	ANGELOU	ART	GLASS
COPS	DRACULA	ANDY	NECKLACE	LAB
BUNNY	DONUTS	FREE SPACE	LIBRARY	STALL
CLOSET	PICASSO	KEEN	MODEL	IT
NECK	RACHEL	CLOWNS	FRIENDS	TENNIS

Speak

MISS	SUFFRAGETTES	MERRYWEATHER	NOTES	GLOBE
SPEAK	BONES	EFFERTS	IVY	BIKE
FREEMAN	DAVID	FREE SPACE	PROM	MARTHAS
LIPS	TAXI	MELINDA	MASCOT	TREE
TENNIS	FRIENDS	CLOWNS	RACHEL	NECK

Speak

BIKE	MELINDA	SEEDS	DRACULA	ANGELOU
MISS	MODEL	NOTES	TENNIS	STALL
FRIENDS	PICASSO	FREE SPACE	NECK	GLASS
MARTHAS	TAXI	LIBRARY	DAVID	BUNNY
BONES	SUFFRAGETTES	MASCOT	COPS	IT

Speak

ART	TREE	PROM	FREEMAN	DONUTS
CLOWNS	LIPS	CLOSET	GLOBE	MERRYWEATHER
ANDY	KEEN	FREE SPACE	EFFERTS	RACHEL
HEATHER	IVY	NICOLE	FROG	SPEAK
IT	COPS	MASCOT	SUFFRAGETTES	BONES

Speak

IT	DRACULA	PICASSO	NECK	CLOWNS
MARTHAS	MELINDA	BUNNY	NICOLE	HEATHER
LIBRARY	GLASS	FREE SPACE	KEEN	COPS
FRIENDS	IVY	MODEL	SPEAK	SEEDS
BIKE	TREE	LAB	ANGELOU	LIPS

Speak

NOTES	SUFFRAGETTES	STALL	BONES	ANDY
TAXI	DONUTS	NECKLACE	ART	EFFERTS
MERRYWEATHER	MASCOT	FREE SPACE	RACHEL	FROG
MISS	GLOBE	DAVID	TENNIS	FREEMAN
LIPS	ANGELOU	LAB	TREE	BIKE

Speak

FROG	HEATHER	IVY	NECKLACE	MODEL
BIKE	SEEDS	MASCOT	GLASS	KEEN
LIBRARY	ANGELOU	FREE SPACE	ART	LIPS
SUFFRAGETTES	NOTES	DAVID	DRACULA	PICASSO
FREEMAN	IT	MARTHAS	NICOLE	PROM

Speak

CLOWNS	NECK	CLOSET	MISS	ANDY
TAXI	STALL	SPEAK	BUNNY	MELINDA
COPS	DONUTS	FREE SPACE	FRIENDS	TENNIS
GLOBE	LAB	RACHEL	TREE	BONES
PROM	NICOLE	MARTHAS	IT	FREEMAN

Speak

SUFFRAGETTES	MERRYWEATHER	GLASS	FREEMAN	NECK
TREE	DAVID	MASCOT	ANGELOU	MISS
CLOWNS	LIBRARY	FREE SPACE	NICOLE	MELINDA
FROG	NECKLACE	STALL	IT	SPEAK
BONES	RACHEL	PROM	IVY	MARTHAS

Speak

MODEL	COPS	TAXI	CLOSET	BUNNY
KEEN	NOTES	LIPS	LAB	EFFERTS
HEATHER	DONUTS	FREE SPACE	FRIENDS	BIKE
GLOBE	PICASSO	TENNIS	SEEDS	DRACULA
MARTHAS	IVY	PROM	RACHEL	BONES

Speak

IT	DONUTS	CLOWNS	TAXI	FROG
LAB	FREEMAN	CLOSET	BIKE	NICOLE
PROM	COPS	FREE SPACE	GLASS	MODEL
MISS	STALL	MERRYWEATHER	KEEN	ANGELOU
BUNNY	GLOBE	IVY	NOTES	NECKLACE

Speak

LIPS	TREE	MARTHAS	SUFFRAGETTES	SEEDS
ART	ANDY	RACHEL	BONES	MELINDA
NECK	FRIENDS	FREE SPACE	SPEAK	PICASSO
LIBRARY	EFFERTS	DRACULA	HEATHER	DAVID
NECKLACE	NOTES	IVY	GLOBE	BUNNY

Speak

FREEMAN	HEATHER	STALL	PROM	DONUTS
GLOBE	BIKE	MODEL	SPEAK	LIBRARY
COPS	LIPS	FREE SPACE	CLOWNS	SUFFRAGETTES
MARTHAS	CLOSET	MISS	GLASS	LAB
DRACULA	PICASSO	NOTES	IVY	RACHEL

Speak

NICOLE	NECK	NECKLACE	MELINDA	TENNIS
IT	TAXI	ANGELOU	ANDY	SEEDS
KEEN	MASCOT	FREE SPACE	BONES	FRIENDS
MERRYWEATHER	TREE	ART	EFFERTS	BUNNY
RACHEL	IVY	NOTES	PICASSO	DRACULA

Speak

TREE	FROG	NICOLE	SUFFRAGETTES	GLASS
BONES	FRIENDS	NOTES	DONUTS	MERRYWEATHER
KEEN	SPEAK	FREE SPACE	FREEMAN	RACHEL
ART	IVY	LAB	DAVID	NECKLACE
CLOWNS	MELINDA	TAXI	IT	COPS

Speak

NECK	SEEDS	ANGELOU	STALL	MASCOT
TENNIS	DRACULA	MARTHAS	GLOBE	PROM
EFFERTS	HEATHER	FREE SPACE	MISS	LIBRARY
BUNNY	CLOSET	ANDY	PICASSO	LIPS
COPS	IT	TAXI	MELINDA	CLOWNS

Speak

MELINDA	IVY	TENNIS	SPEAK	MERRYWEATHER
CLOWNS	PROM	STALL	LAB	MASCOT
DONUTS	NECKLACE	FREE SPACE	DAVID	DRACULA
BIKE	NICOLE	MISS	FROG	NECK
NOTES	GLOBE	LIBRARY	RACHEL	SEEDS

Speak

FRIENDS	SUFFRAGETTES	FREEMAN	COPS	ANDY
BONES	PICASSO	IT	TAXI	TREE
GLASS	KEEN	FREE SPACE	LIPS	ART
MARTHAS	EFFERTS	BUNNY	ANGELOU	HEATHER
SEEDS	RACHEL	LIBRARY	GLOBE	NOTES

Speak

PROM	IT	LIBRARY	MELINDA	EFFERTS
CLOWNS	LAB	RACHEL	MERRYWEATHER	BIKE
ANDY	FROG	FREE SPACE	DRACULA	NECK
MISS	MASCOT	BUNNY	STALL	NECKLACE
ART	BONES	PICASSO	IVY	KEEN

Speak

TREE	GLOBE	SEEDS	FRIENDS	SUFFRAGETTES
LIPS	MARTHAS	SPEAK	COPS	FREEMAN
DONUTS	GLASS	FREE SPACE	NOTES	NICOLE
TENNIS	MODEL	CLOSET	TAXI	ANGELOU
KEEN	IVY	PICASSO	BONES	ART

Speak

FREEMAN	ANGELOU	MERRYWEATHER	KEEN	NOTES
DONUTS	GLOBE	ANDY	STALL	SPEAK
CLOSET	IVY	FREE SPACE	MODEL	CLOWNS
ART	TREE	HEATHER	NECKLACE	RACHEL
GLASS	DRACULA	NECK	MASCOT	MELINDA

Speak

TENNIS	BUNNY	BONES	COPS	EFFERTS
LIPS	SEEDS	MISS	PROM	LIBRARY
PICASSO	SUFFRAGETTES	FREE SPACE	DAVID	FRIENDS
NICOLE	MARTHAS	TAXI	IT	LAB
MELINDA	MASCOT	NECK	DRACULA	GLASS

Speak Vocabulary Word List

No.	Word	Clue/Definition
1.	ALLEGEDLY	Supposedly; put forth as true but not proven
2.	ASPHYXIATED	Suffocated; smothered; choked
3.	BANISHED	Forced to leave
4.	BIGOTED	Intolerant of any other beliefs or opinions
5.	BURROW	Hole or hideout animals use to take shelter
6.	COAXES	Persuades by pleading or flattery
7.	CONSCIENCE	Inner sense of what is right or wrong
8.	CONSISTENCY	Keeping the same behavior, form, pattern, or principles
9.	CONUNDRUM	Difficult problem; dilemma
10.	DEGRADING	Humiliating; disgracing
11.	DELINQUENCY	Failure to fulfill a duty or obligation; something wrongful or illegal
12.	DEMERIT	Mark against someone for misconduct
13.	DEMURE	Shy; modest; coy
14.	DENSE	Dull or slow-witted
15.	DEVIOUS	Deceitful; not straightforward
16.	DORMANT	Inactive; asleep
17.	DRONE	Remote-controlled mechanism
18.	DYNAMICS	Social, intellectual, or physical forces that characterize a system or group
19.	ERRANT	Straying from the right course
20.	FLOUNDERING	Acting clumsily or in confusion
21.	FOSTER	Something that nourishes or cares for
22.	GENETICS	Science of heredity and genes
23.	HAZING	Abusing newcomers with humiliating tricks and ridicule before they become a part of the group
24.	IMBECILES	Stupid or silly people
25.	INCITING	Stirring up (trouble); egging-on
26.	INCONSPICUOUS	Not noticeable
27.	INCRIMINATE	Make someone appear guilty of a crime
28.	INDOCTRINATION	Teaching someone to accept an idea or principle without criticism
29.	LEPER	Outcast
30.	MALADJUSTED	Not in sync with one's circumstances
31.	MOMENTUM	Force or speed of movement
32.	MUSE	Something or someone that is inspiring to an artist
33.	PRUNING	Cutting; clipping
34.	PSEUDO	Fake; false; pretend
35.	RECESSIVE	Going to the back; a gene that does not produce
36.	REFURBISHED	Made clean, bright, or fresh again
37.	RELUCTANCE	Unwillingness; resistance
38.	REPUTATION	How the public views or regards an individual
39.	RETREAT	Withdraw; go back
40.	REVOLUTIONARY	Supporting radical change or innovation
41.	SANCTUARY	Sacred place offering refuge or safety
42.	SENSIBILITIES	Emotions; feelings
43.	SUBJECTIVITY	Based on personal feelings rather than facts
44.	SUBMISSION	Surrendering power to another
45.	TENACIOUS	Persistent; stubborn; won't give up
46.	VAGUELY	Not clear or definite
47.	VESPIARY	Nest of social wasps
48.	WAN	Pale in color; sickly-looking
49.	WISTFUL	Thoughtful in a sad way; longing

Speak Vocabulary Word List Continued

No.	Word	Clue/Definition
50.	XENOPHOBIC	Having an unreasonable fear or hatred of foreigners

Speak Vocabulary Fill In The Blanks 1

1. Persuades by pleading or flattery
2. Sacred place offering refuge or safety
3. Going to the back; a gene that does not produce
4. Inactive; asleep
5. Based on personal feelings rather than facts
6. Stupid or silly people
7. Inner sense of what is right or wrong
8. Unwillingness; resistance
9. Persistent; stubborn; won't give up
10. Supporting radical change or innovation
11. Acting clumsily or in confusion
12. Something or someone that is inspiring to an artist
13. Keeping the same behavior, form, pattern, or principles
14. Force or speed of movement
15. Emotions; feelings
16. Mark against someone for misconduct
17. Straying from the right course
18. Abusing newcomers with humiliating tricks and ridicule before they become a part of the group
19. Deceitful; not straightforward
20. Suffocated; smothered; choked

Speak Vocabulary Fill In The Blanks 1 Answer Key

COAXES	1. Persuades by pleading or flattery
SANCTUARY	2. Sacred place offering refuge or safety
RECESSIVE	3. Going to the back; a gene that does not produce
DORMANT	4. Inactive; asleep
SUBJECTIVITY	5. Based on personal feelings rather than facts
IMBECILES	6. Stupid or silly people
CONSCIENCE	7. Inner sense of what is right or wrong
RELUCTANCE	8. Unwillingness; resistance
TENACIOUS	9. Persistent; stubborn; won't give up
REVOLUTIONARY	10. Supporting radical change or innovation
FLOUNDERING	11. Acting clumsily or in confusion
MUSE	12. Something or someone that is inspiring to an artist
CONSISTENCY	13. Keeping the same behavior, form, pattern, or principles
MOMENTUM	14. Force or speed of movement
SENSIBILITIES	15. Emotions; feelings
DEMERIT	16. Mark against someone for misconduct
ERRANT	17. Straying from the right course
HAZING	18. Abusing newcomers with humiliating tricks and ridicule before they become a part of the group
DEVIOUS	19. Deceitful; not straightforward
ASPHYXIATED	20. Suffocated; smothered; choked

Speak Vocabulary Fill In The Blanks 2

1. Emotions; feelings
2. Straying from the right course
3. Forced to leave
4. Abusing newcomers with humiliating tricks and ridicule before they become a part of the group
5. Cutting; clipping
6. Keeping the same behavior, form, pattern, or principles
7. Difficult problem; dilemma
8. Dull or slow-witted
9. Going to the back; a gene that does not produce
10. Unwillingness; resistance
11. Pale in color; sickly-looking
12. Acting clumsily or in confusion
13. Hole or hideout animals use to take shelter
14. Stirring up (trouble); egging-on
15. Surrendering power to another
16. Persistent; stubborn; won't give up
17. Make someone appear guilty of a crime
18. Science of heredity and genes
19. Something or someone that is inspiring to an artist
20. How the public views or regards an individual

Speak Vocabulary Fill In The Blanks 2 Answer Key

SENSIBILITIES	1.	Emotions; feelings
ERRANT	2.	Straying from the right course
BANISHED	3.	Forced to leave
HAZING	4.	Abusing newcomers with humiliating tricks and ridicule before they become a part of the group
PRUNING	5.	Cutting; clipping
CONSISTENCY	6.	Keeping the same behavior, form, pattern, or principles
CONUNDRUM	7.	Difficult problem; dilemma
DENSE	8.	Dull or slow-witted
RECESSIVE	9.	Going to the back; a gene that does not produce
RELUCTANCE	10.	Unwillingness; resistance
WAN	11.	Pale in color; sickly-looking
FLOUNDERING	12.	Acting clumsily or in confusion
BURROW	13.	Hole or hideout animals use to take shelter
INCITING	14.	Stirring up (trouble); egging-on
SUBMISSION	15.	Surrendering power to another
TENACIOUS	16.	Persistent; stubborn; won't give up
INCRIMINATE	17.	Make someone appear guilty of a crime
GENETICS	18.	Science of heredity and genes
MUSE	19.	Something or someone that is inspiring to an artist
REPUTATION	20.	How the public views or regards an individual

Speak Vocabulary Fill In The Blanks 3

1. Withdraw; go back
2. Surrendering power to another
3. Having an unreasonable fear or hatred of foreigners
4. Shy; modest; coy
5. Supporting radical change or innovation
6. Straying from the right course
7. Made clean, bright, or fresh again
8. Acting clumsily or in confusion
9. Not noticeable
10. Something or someone that is inspiring to an artist
11. Supposedly; put forth as true but not proven
12. Difficult problem; dilemma
13. Going to the back; a gene that does not produce
14. Science of heredity and genes
15. Cutting; clipping
16. Force or speed of movement
17. Persuades by pleading or flattery
18. Outcast
19. Suffocated; smothered; choked
20. Thoughtful in a sad way; longing

Speak Vocabulary Fill In The Blanks 3 Answer Key

RETREAT	1. Withdraw; go back
SUBMISSION	2. Surrendering power to another
XENOPHOBIC	3. Having an unreasonable fear or hatred of foreigners
DEMURE	4. Shy; modest; coy
REVOLUTIONARY	5. Supporting radical change or innovation
ERRANT	6. Straying from the right course
REFURBISHED	7. Made clean, bright, or fresh again
FLOUNDERING	8. Acting clumsily or in confusion
INCONSPICUOUS	9. Not noticeable
MUSE	10. Something or someone that is inspiring to an artist
ALLEGEDLY	11. Supposedly; put forth as true but not proven
CONUNDRUM	12. Difficult problem; dilemma
RECESSIVE	13. Going to the back; a gene that does not produce
GENETICS	14. Science of heredity and genes
PRUNING	15. Cutting; clipping
MOMENTUM	16. Force or speed of movement
COAXES	17. Persuades by pleading or flattery
LEPER	18. Outcast
ASPHYXIATED	19. Suffocated; smothered; choked
WISTFUL	20. Thoughtful in a sad way; longing

Speak Vocabulary Fill In The Blanks 4

1. Fake; false; pretend
2. Stirring up (trouble); egging-on
3. Intolerant of any other beliefs or opinions
4. Not in sync with one's circumstances
5. Stupid or silly people
6. How the public views or regards an individual
7. Inner sense of what is right or wrong
8. Social, intellectual, or physical forces that characterize a system or group
9. Persistent; stubborn; won't give up
10. Mark against someone for misconduct
11. Difficult problem; dilemma
12. Made clean, bright, or fresh again
13. Emotions; feelings
14. Shy; modest; coy
15. Make someone appear guilty of a crime
16. Surrendering power to another
17. Supporting radical change or innovation
18. Unwillingness; resistance
19. Going to the back; a gene that does not produce
20. Inactive; asleep

Speak Vocabulary Fill In The Blanks 4 Answer Key

PSEUDO	1. Fake; false; pretend
INCITING	2. Stirring up (trouble); egging-on
BIGOTED	3. Intolerant of any other beliefs or opinions
MALADJUSTED	4. Not in sync with one's circumstances
IMBECILES	5. Stupid or silly people
REPUTATION	6. How the public views or regards an individual
CONSCIENCE	7. Inner sense of what is right or wrong
DYNAMICS	8. Social, intellectual, or physical forces that characterize a system or group
TENACIOUS	9. Persistent; stubborn; won't give up
DEMERIT	10. Mark against someone for misconduct
CONUNDRUM	11. Difficult problem; dilemma
REFURBISHED	12. Made clean, bright, or fresh again
SENSIBILITIES	13. Emotions; feelings
DEMURE	14. Shy; modest; coy
INCRIMINATE	15. Make someone appear guilty of a crime
SUBMISSION	16. Surrendering power to another
REVOLUTIONARY	17. Supporting radical change or innovation
RELUCTANCE	18. Unwillingness; resistance
RECESSIVE	19. Going to the back; a gene that does not produce
DORMANT	20. Inactive; asleep

Speak Vocabulary Matching 1

___ 1. LEPER A. Something or someone that is inspiring to an artist
___ 2. RELUCTANCE B. Not in sync with one's circumstances
___ 3. WISTFUL C. Outcast
___ 4. ASPHYXIATED D. Forced to leave
___ 5. SENSIBILITIES E. Cutting; clipping
___ 6. DENSE F. Suffocated; smothered; choked
___ 7. BIGOTED G. Persistent; stubborn; won't give up
___ 8. XENOPHOBIC H. Hole or hideout animals use to take shelter
___ 9. SUBMISSION I. How the public views or regards an individual
___ 10. CONSCIENCE J. Teaching someone to accept an idea or principle without criticism
___ 11. MALADJUSTED K. Force or speed of movement
___ 12. MUSE L. Mark against someone for misconduct
___ 13. WAN M. Surrendering power to another
___ 14. ALLEGEDLY N. Pale in color; sickly-looking
___ 15. TENACIOUS O. Having an unreasonable fear or hatred of foreigners
___ 16. REPUTATION P. Intolerant of any other beliefs or opinions
___ 17. MOMENTUM Q. Supposedly; put forth as true but not proven
___ 18. INCONSPICUOUS R. Stupid or silly people
___ 19. PSEUDO S. Unwillingness; resistance
___ 20. BANISHED T. Fake; false; pretend
___ 21. DEMERIT U. Not noticeable
___ 22. IMBECILES V. Dull or slow-witted
___ 23. BURROW W. Inner sense of what is right or wrong
___ 24. PRUNING X. Thoughtful in a sad way; longing
___ 25. INDOCTRINATION Y. Emotions; feelings

Speak Vocabulary Matching 1 Answer Key

C - 1. LEPER	A.	Something or someone that is inspiring to an artist
S - 2. RELUCTANCE	B.	Not in sync with one's circumstances
X - 3. WISTFUL	C.	Outcast
F - 4. ASPHYXIATED	D.	Forced to leave
Y - 5. SENSIBILITIES	E.	Cutting; clipping
V - 6. DENSE	F.	Suffocated; smothered; choked
P - 7. BIGOTED	G.	Persistent; stubborn; won't give up
O - 8. XENOPHOBIC	H.	Hole or hideout animals use to take shelter
M - 9. SUBMISSION	I.	How the public views or regards an individual
W - 10. CONSCIENCE	J.	Teaching someone to accept an idea or principle without criticism
B - 11. MALADJUSTED	K.	Force or speed of movement
A - 12. MUSE	L.	Mark against someone for misconduct
N - 13. WAN	M.	Surrendering power to another
Q - 14. ALLEGEDLY	N.	Pale in color; sickly-looking
G - 15. TENACIOUS	O.	Having an unreasonable fear or hatred of foreigners
I - 16. REPUTATION	P.	Intolerant of any other beliefs or opinions
K - 17. MOMENTUM	Q.	Supposedly; put forth as true but not proven
U - 18. INCONSPICUOUS	R.	Stupid or silly people
T - 19. PSEUDO	S.	Unwillingness; resistance
D - 20. BANISHED	T.	Fake; false; pretend
L - 21. DEMERIT	U.	Not noticeable
R - 22. IMBECILES	V.	Dull or slow-witted
H - 23. BURROW	W.	Inner sense of what is right or wrong
E - 24. PRUNING	X.	Thoughtful in a sad way; longing
J - 25. INDOCTRINATION	Y.	Emotions; feelings

Speak Vocabulary Matching 2

___ 1. DORMANT
___ 2. GENETICS
___ 3. SUBMISSION
___ 4. SENSIBILITIES
___ 5. DELINQUENCY
___ 6. ALLEGEDLY
___ 7. MALADJUSTED
___ 8. RETREAT
___ 9. BIGOTED
___ 10. ASPHYXIATED
___ 11. TENACIOUS
___ 12. REFURBISHED
___ 13. RELUCTANCE
___ 14. DEMURE
___ 15. DYNAMICS
___ 16. HAZING
___ 17. PSEUDO
___ 18. PRUNING
___ 19. CONUNDRUM
___ 20. SUBJECTIVITY
___ 21. ERRANT
___ 22. FOSTER
___ 23. DEVIOUS
___ 24. FLOUNDERING
___ 25. SANCTUARY

A. Emotions; feelings
B. Surrendering power to another
C. Inactive; asleep
D. Failure to fulfill a duty or obligation; something wrongful or illegal
E. Something that nourishes or cares for
F. Fake; false; pretend
G. Science of heredity and genes
H. Social, intellectual, or physical forces that characterize a system or group
I. Based on personal feelings rather than facts
J. Sacred place offering refuge or safety
K. Unwillingness; resistance
L. Abusing newcomers with humiliating tricks and ridicule before they become a part of the group
M. Deceitful; not straightforward
N. Cutting; clipping
O. Intolerant of any other beliefs or opinions
P. Straying from the right course
Q. Withdraw; go back
R. Made clean, bright, or fresh again
S. Persistent; stubborn; won't give up
T. Acting clumsily or in confusion
U. Suffocated; smothered; choked
V. Supposedly; put forth as true but not proven
W. Shy; modest; coy
X. Not in sync with one's circumstances
Y. Difficult problem; dilemma

Speak Vocabulary Matching 2 Answer Key

C - 1.	DORMANT	A. Emotions; feelings
G - 2.	GENETICS	B. Surrendering power to another
B - 3.	SUBMISSION	C. Inactive; asleep
A - 4.	SENSIBILITIES	D. Failure to fulfill a duty or obligation; something wrongful or illegal
D - 5.	DELINQUENCY	E. Something that nourishes or cares for
V - 6.	ALLEGEDLY	F. Fake; false; pretend
X - 7.	MALADJUSTED	G. Science of heredity and genes
Q - 8.	RETREAT	H. Social, intellectual, or physical forces that characterize a system or group
O - 9.	BIGOTED	I. Based on personal feelings rather than facts
U - 10.	ASPHYXIATED	J. Sacred place offering refuge or safety
S - 11.	TENACIOUS	K. Unwillingness; resistance
R - 12.	REFURBISHED	L. Abusing newcomers with humiliating tricks and ridicule before they become a part of the group
K - 13.	RELUCTANCE	M. Deceitful; not straightforward
W - 14.	DEMURE	N. Cutting; clipping
H - 15.	DYNAMICS	O. Intolerant of any other beliefs or opinions
L - 16.	HAZING	P. Straying from the right course
F - 17.	PSEUDO	Q. Withdraw; go back
N - 18.	PRUNING	R. Made clean, bright, or fresh again
Y - 19.	CONUNDRUM	S. Persistent; stubborn; won't give up
I - 20.	SUBJECTIVITY	T. Acting clumsily or in confusion
P - 21.	ERRANT	U. Suffocated; smothered; choked
E - 22.	FOSTER	V. Supposedly; put forth as true but not proven
M - 23.	DEVIOUS	W. Shy; modest; coy
T - 24.	FLOUNDERING	X. Not in sync with one's circumstances
J - 25.	SANCTUARY	Y. Difficult problem; dilemma

Speak Vocabulary Matching 3

___ 1. BIGOTED
___ 2. BANISHED
___ 3. LEPER
___ 4. DENSE
___ 5. ERRANT
___ 6. INDOCTRINATION
___ 7. DEVIOUS
___ 8. HAZING
___ 9. TENACIOUS
___ 10. RELUCTANCE
___ 11. BURROW
___ 12. PRUNING
___ 13. SENSIBILITIES
___ 14. DYNAMICS
___ 15. CONSCIENCE
___ 16. VAGUELY
___ 17. XENOPHOBIC
___ 18. SUBMISSION
___ 19. CONSISTENCY
___ 20. INCRIMINATE
___ 21. WAN
___ 22. COAXES
___ 23. DEMURE
___ 24. INCONSPICUOUS
___ 25. DEMERIT

A. Emotions; feelings
B. Inner sense of what is right or wrong
C. Not clear or definite
D. Forced to leave
E. Dull or slow-witted
F. Outcast
G. Having an unreasonable fear or hatred of foreigners
H. Keeping the same behavior, form, pattern, or principles
I. Mark against someone for misconduct
J. Cutting; clipping
K. Teaching someone to accept an idea or principle without criticism
L. Unwillingness; resistance
M. Persuades by pleading or flattery
N. Social, intellectual, or physical forces that characterize a system or group
O. Persistent; stubborn; won't give up
P. Pale in color; sickly-looking
Q. Hole or hideout animals use to take shelter
R. Deceitful; not straightforward
S. Abusing newcomers with humiliating tricks and ridicule before they become a part of the group
T. Surrendering power to another
U. Straying from the right course
V. Not noticeable
W. Shy; modest; coy
X. Intolerant of any other beliefs or opinions
Y. Make someone appear guilty of a crime

Speak Vocabulary Matching 3 Answer Key

X - 1.	BIGOTED	A. Emotions; feelings
D - 2.	BANISHED	B. Inner sense of what is right or wrong
F - 3.	LEPER	C. Not clear or definite
E - 4.	DENSE	D. Forced to leave
U - 5.	ERRANT	E. Dull or slow-witted
K - 6.	INDOCTRINATION	F. Outcast
R - 7.	DEVIOUS	G. Having an unreasonable fear or hatred of foreigners
S - 8.	HAZING	H. Keeping the same behavior, form, pattern, or principles
O - 9.	TENACIOUS	I. Mark against someone for misconduct
L - 10.	RELUCTANCE	J. Cutting; clipping
Q - 11.	BURROW	K. Teaching someone to accept an idea or principle without criticism
J - 12.	PRUNING	L. Unwillingness; resistance
A - 13.	SENSIBILITIES	M. Persuades by pleading or flattery
N - 14.	DYNAMICS	N. Social, intellectual, or physical forces that characterize a system or group
B - 15.	CONSCIENCE	O. Persistent; stubborn; won't give up
C - 16.	VAGUELY	P. Pale in color; sickly-looking
G - 17.	XENOPHOBIC	Q. Hole or hideout animals use to take shelter
T - 18.	SUBMISSION	R. Deceitful; not straightforward
H - 19.	CONSISTENCY	S. Abusing newcomers with humiliating tricks and ridicule before they become a part of the group
Y - 20.	INCRIMINATE	T. Surrendering power to another
P - 21.	WAN	U. Straying from the right course
M - 22.	COAXES	V. Not noticeable
W - 23.	DEMURE	W. Shy; modest; coy
V - 24.	INCONSPICUOUS	X. Intolerant of any other beliefs or opinions
I - 25.	DEMERIT	Y. Make someone appear guilty of a crime

Speak Vocabulary Matching 4

___ 1. FOSTER
___ 2. INCRIMINATE
___ 3. ALLEGEDLY
___ 4. DYNAMICS
___ 5. VAGUELY
___ 6. WAN
___ 7. MUSE
___ 8. SANCTUARY
___ 9. BURROW
___ 10. SUBMISSION
___ 11. DELINQUENCY
___ 12. PSEUDO
___ 13. DEVIOUS
___ 14. INCITING
___ 15. REVOLUTIONARY
___ 16. DEMURE
___ 17. TENACIOUS
___ 18. DEGRADING
___ 19. RETREAT
___ 20. VESPIARY
___ 21. CONSCIENCE
___ 22. INCONSPICUOUS
___ 23. GENETICS
___ 24. COAXES
___ 25. MOMENTUM

A. Surrendering power to another
B. Not noticeable
C. Failure to fulfill a duty or obligation; something wrongful or illegal
D. Persistent; stubborn; won't give up
E. Fake; false; pretend
F. Science of heredity and genes
G. Supposedly; put forth as true but not proven
H. Force or speed of movement
I. Shy; modest; coy
J. Supporting radical change or innovation
K. Humiliating; disgracing
L. Nest of social wasps
M. Deceitful; not straightforward
N. Hole or hideout animals use to take shelter
O. Something that nourishes or cares for
P. Sacred place offering refuge or safety
Q. Not clear or definite
R. Persuades by pleading or flattery
S. Pale in color; sickly-looking
T. Inner sense of what is right or wrong
U. Make someone appear guilty of a crime
V. Social, intellectual, or physical forces that characterize a system or group
W. Something or someone that is inspiring to an artist
X. Stirring up (trouble); egging-on
Y. Withdraw; go back

Speak Vocabulary Matching 4 Answer Key

O - 1.	FOSTER	A. Surrendering power to another
U - 2.	INCRIMINATE	B. Not noticeable
G - 3.	ALLEGEDLY	C. Failure to fulfill a duty or obligation; something wrongful or illegal
V - 4.	DYNAMICS	D. Persistent; stubborn; won't give up
Q - 5.	VAGUELY	E. Fake; false; pretend
S - 6.	WAN	F. Science of heredity and genes
W - 7.	MUSE	G. Supposedly; put forth as true but not proven
P - 8.	SANCTUARY	H. Force or speed of movement
N - 9.	BURROW	I. Shy; modest; coy
A - 10.	SUBMISSION	J. Supporting radical change or innovation
C - 11.	DELINQUENCY	K. Humiliating; disgracing
E - 12.	PSEUDO	L. Nest of social wasps
M - 13.	DEVIOUS	M. Deceitful; not straightforward
X - 14.	INCITING	N. Hole or hideout animals use to take shelter
J - 15.	REVOLUTIONARY	O. Something that nourishes or cares for
I - 16.	DEMURE	P. Sacred place offering refuge or safety
D - 17.	TENACIOUS	Q. Not clear or definite
K - 18.	DEGRADING	R. Persuades by pleading or flattery
Y - 19.	RETREAT	S. Pale in color; sickly-looking
L - 20.	VESPIARY	T. Inner sense of what is right or wrong
T - 21.	CONSCIENCE	U. Make someone appear guilty of a crime
B - 22.	INCONSPICUOUS	V. Social, intellectual, or physical forces that characterize a system or group
F - 23.	GENETICS	W. Something or someone that is inspiring to an artist
R - 24.	COAXES	X. Stirring up (trouble); egging-on
H - 25.	MOMENTUM	Y. Withdraw; go back

Speak Vocabulary Magic Squares 1

Match the definition with the vocabulary word. Put your answers in the magic squares below. When your answers are correct, all columns and rows will add to the same number.

A. DELINQUENCY
B. SANCTUARY
C. FOSTER
D. CONSCIENCE
E. VESPIARY
F. DRONE
G. WISTFUL
H. REFURBISHED
I. DENSE
J. VAGUELY
K. HAZING
L. RETREAT
M. INCITING
N. TENACIOUS
O. BURROW
P. XENOPHOBIC

1. Remote-controlled mechanism
2. Dull or slow-witted
3. Hole or hideout animals use to take shelter
4. Inner sense of what is right or wrong
5. Stirring up (trouble); egging-on
6. Sacred place offering refuge or safety
7. Made clean, bright, or fresh again
8. Abusing newcomers with humiliating tricks and ridicule before they become a part of the group
9. Something that nourishes or cares for
10. Having an unreasonable fear or hatred of foreigners
11. Not clear or definite
12. Nest of social wasps
13. Withdraw; go back
14. Thoughtful in a sad way; longing
15. Failure to fulfill a duty or obligation; something wrongful or illegal
16. Persistent; stubborn; won't give up

A=	B=	C=	D=
E=	F=	G=	H=
I=	J=	K=	L=
M=	N=	O=	P=

Speak Vocabulary Magic Squares 1 Answer Key

Match the definition with the vocabulary word. Put your answers in the magic squares below. When your answers are correct, all columns and rows will add to the same number.

A. DELINQUENCY
B. SANCTUARY
C. FOSTER
D. CONSCIENCE
E. VESPIARY
F. DRONE
G. WISTFUL
H. REFURBISHED
I. DENSE
J. VAGUELY
K. HAZING
L. RETREAT
M. INCITING
N. TENACIOUS
O. BURROW
P. XENOPHOBIC

1. Remote-controlled mechanism
2. Dull or slow-witted
3. Hole or hideout animals use to take shelter
4. Inner sense of what is right or wrong
5. Stirring up (trouble); egging-on
6. Sacred place offering refuge or safety
7. Made clean, bright, or fresh again
8. Abusing newcomers with humiliating tricks and ridicule before they become a part of the group
9. Something that nourishes or cares for
10. Having an unreasonable fear or hatred of foreigners
11. Not clear or definite
12. Nest of social wasps
13. Withdraw; go back
14. Thoughtful in a sad way; longing
15. Failure to fulfill a duty or obligation; something wrongful or illegal
16. Persistent; stubborn; won't give up

A=15	B=6	C=9	D=4
E=12	F=1	G=14	H=7
I=2	J=11	K=8	L=13
M=5	N=16	O=3	P=10

Speak Vocabulary Magic Squares 2

Match the definition with the vocabulary word. Put your answers in the magic squares below. When your answers are correct, all columns and rows will add to the same number.

A. PSEUDO
B. LEPER
C. XENOPHOBIC
D. INCONSPICUOUS
E. ERRANT
F. PRUNING
G. DORMANT
H. REFURBISHED
I. SANCTUARY
J. GENETICS
K. DYNAMICS
L. REVOLUTIONARY
M. ASPHYXIATED
N. SENSIBILITIES
O. TENACIOUS
P. VAGUELY

1. Having an unreasonable fear or hatred of foreigners
2. Science of heredity and genes
3. Cutting; clipping
4. Persistent; stubborn; won't give up
5. Not clear or definite
6. Straying from the right course
7. Sacred place offering refuge or safety
8. Not noticeable
9. Suffocated; smothered; choked
10. Made clean, bright, or fresh again
11. Supporting radical change or innovation
12. Fake; false; pretend
13. Outcast
14. Social, intellectual, or physical forces that characterize a system or group
15. Inactive; asleep
16. Emotions; feelings

A=	B=	C=	D=
E=	F=	G=	H=
I=	J=	K=	L=
M=	N=	O=	P=

Speak Vocabulary Magic Squares 2 Answer Key

Match the definition with the vocabulary word. Put your answers in the magic squares below. When your answers are correct, all columns and rows will add to the same number.

A. PSEUDO
B. LEPER
C. XENOPHOBIC
D. INCONSPICUOUS
E. ERRANT
F. PRUNING
G. DORMANT
H. REFURBISHED
I. SANCTUARY
J. GENETICS
K. DYNAMICS
L. REVOLUTIONARY
M. ASPHYXIATED
N. SENSIBILITIES
O. TENACIOUS
P. VAGUELY

1. Having an unreasonable fear or hatred of foreigners
2. Science of heredity and genes
3. Cutting; clipping
4. Persistent; stubborn; won't give up
5. Not clear or definite
6. Straying from the right course
7. Sacred place offering refuge or safety
8. Not noticeable
9. Suffocated; smothered; choked
10. Made clean, bright, or fresh again
11. Supporting radical change or innovation
12. Fake; false; pretend
13. Outcast
14. Social, intellectual, or physical forces that characterize a system or group
15. Inactive; asleep
16. Emotions; feelings

A=12	B=13	C=1	D=8
E=6	F=3	G=15	H=10
I=7	J=2	K=14	L=11
M=9	N=16	O=4	P=5

Speak Vocabulary Magic Squares 3

Match the definition with the vocabulary word. Put your answers in the magic squares below. When your answers are correct, all columns and rows will add to the same number.

A. INCITING
B. ERRANT
C. PSEUDO
D. FLOUNDERING
E. DYNAMICS
F. DEGRADING
G. RELUCTANCE
H. DELINQUENCY
I. HAZING
J. CONSISTENCY
K. DORMANT
L. IMBECILES
M. ASPHYXIATED
N. MOMENTUM
O. DEMERIT
P. PRUNING

1. Mark against someone for misconduct
2. Acting clumsily or in confusion
3. Keeping the same behavior, form, pattern, or principles
4. Social, intellectual, or physical forces that characterize a system or group
5. Abusing newcomers with humiliating tricks and ridicule before they become a part of the group
6. Humiliating; disgracing
7. Cutting; clipping
8. Fake; false; pretend
9. Failure to fulfill a duty or obligation; something wrongful or illegal
10. Inactive; asleep
11. Stirring up (trouble); egging-on
12. Force or speed of movement
13. Straying from the right course
14. Suffocated; smothered; choked
15. Unwillingness; resistance
16. Stupid or silly people

A= 11	B= 13	C= 8	D= 2
E= 4	F= 6	G= 15	H= 9
I= 5	J= 3	K= 10	L= 16
M= 14	N= 12	O= 1	P= 7

Speak Vocabulary Magic Squares 3 Answer Key

Match the definition with the vocabulary word. Put your answers in the magic squares below. When your answers are correct, all columns and rows will add to the same number.

A. INCITING
B. ERRANT
C. PSEUDO
D. FLOUNDERING
E. DYNAMICS
F. DEGRADING
G. RELUCTANCE
H. DELINQUENCY
I. HAZING
J. CONSISTENCY
K. DORMANT
L. IMBECILES
M. ASPHYXIATED
N. MOMENTUM
O. DEMERIT
P. PRUNING

1. Mark against someone for misconduct
2. Acting clumsily or in confusion
3. Keeping the same behavior, form, pattern, or principles
4. Social, intellectual, or physical forces that characterize a system or group
5. Abusing newcomers with humiliating tricks and ridicule before they become a part of the group
6. Humiliating; disgracing
7. Cutting; clipping
8. Fake; false; pretend
9. Failure to fulfill a duty or obligation; something wrongful or illegal
10. Inactive; asleep
11. Stirring up (trouble); egging-on
12. Force or speed of movement
13. Straying from the right course
14. Suffocated; smothered; choked
15. Unwillingness; resistance
16. Stupid or silly people

A=11	B=13	C=8	D=2
E=4	F=6	G=15	H=9
I=5	J=3	K=10	L=16
M=14	N=12	O=1	P=7

Speak Vocabulary Magic Squares 4

Match the definition with the vocabulary word. Put your answers in the magic squares below. When your answers are correct, all columns and rows will add to the same number.

A. GENETICS
B. MUSE
C. CONSISTENCY
D. DEMURE
E. RECESSIVE
F. DEVIOUS
G. CONUNDRUM
H. CONSCIENCE
I. SANCTUARY
J. XENOPHOBIC
K. PSEUDO
L. REVOLUTIONARY
M. TENACIOUS
N. HAZING
O. DEMERIT
P. DENSE

1. Something or someone that is inspiring to an artist
2. Difficult problem; dilemma
3. Fake; false; pretend
4. Abusing newcomers with humiliating tricks and ridicule before they become a part of the group
5. Persistent; stubborn; won't give up
6. Supporting radical change or innovation
7. Inner sense of what is right or wrong
8. Science of heredity and genes
9. Dull or slow-witted
10. Sacred place offering refuge or safety
11. Going to the back; a gene that does not produce
12. Shy; modest; coy
13. Keeping the same behavior, form, pattern, or principles
14. Deceitful; not straightforward
15. Having an unreasonable fear or hatred of foreigners
16. Mark against someone for misconduct

A=	B=	C=	D=
E=	F=	G=	H=
I=	J=	K=	L=
M=	N=	O=	P=

Speak Vocabulary Magic Squares 4 Answer Key

Match the definition with the vocabulary word. Put your answers in the magic squares below. When your answers are correct, all columns and rows will add to the same number.

A. GENETICS
B. MUSE
C. CONSISTENCY
D. DEMURE
E. RECESSIVE
F. DEVIOUS
G. CONUNDRUM
H. CONSCIENCE
I. SANCTUARY
J. XENOPHOBIC
K. PSEUDO
L. REVOLUTIONARY
M. TENACIOUS
N. HAZING
O. DEMERIT
P. DENSE

1. Something or someone that is inspiring to an artist
2. Difficult problem; dilemma
3. Fake; false; pretend
4. Abusing newcomers with humiliating tricks and ridicule before they become a part of the group
5. Persistent; stubborn; won't give up
6. Supporting radical change or innovation
7. Inner sense of what is right or wrong
8. Science of heredity and genes
9. Dull or slow-witted
10. Sacred place offering refuge or safety
11. Going to the back; a gene that does not produce
12. Shy; modest; coy
13. Keeping the same behavior, form, pattern, or principles
14. Deceitful; not straightforward
15. Having an unreasonable fear or hatred of foreigners
16. Mark against someone for misconduct

A=8	B=1	C=13	D=12
E=11	F=14	G=2	H=7
I=10	J=15	K=3	L=6
M=5	N=4	O=16	P=9

Speak Vocabulary Word Search 1

```
I N C O N S P I C U O U S F T Y D T
N O I S S I M B U S B T I R E M E D
P N V J U C O N S C I E N C E M P L
R E T S O F K M A C K Z B N K G H P B
L W C Q I G T H N I W A N P S W W E
R Y Y O C N X S C N T A G I B M N K
N O I T A N I R T C O D N I U O K P
G P W M N X H Q U I Z A I R R M D T
Y J R V E B E L A T B S D D R E L X
F O R V T M E S R I W N A A O N E N
D S V Y H R U F Y N B R L L W T R F
I X I A K E Y S S G F E G L Y U R L
N Z M S G F C P E S P C E E T M A K
C W B M G U N X Y E M E D G Y U N F
R P E D E R E P L H E S N E D R T S
I R C Y N B U L J A W S S D E D P Q
M U I N E I Q B Y Z I I U L T N S D
I N L A T S N X V I S V O Y O U E G
N I E M I H I F B N T E I J G N U H
A N S I C E L J Q G F F V N I O D Y
T G Z C S D E D E M U R E T B C O D
E R X S Y R D G R F L C D W D T S M
```

ALLEGEDLY
BANISHED
BIGOTED
BURROW
COAXES
CONSCIENCE
CONUNDRUM
DEGRADING
DELINQUENCY
DEMERIT

DEMURE
DENSE
DEVIOUS
DORMANT
DRONE
DYNAMICS
ERRANT
FOSTER
GENETICS
HAZING

IMBECILES
INCITING
INCONSPICUOUS
INCRIMINATE
INDOCTRINATION
LEPER
MOMENTUM
MUSE
PRUNING
PSEUDO

RECESSIVE
REFURBISHED
RELUCTANCE
SANCTUARY
SUBMISSION
TENACIOUS
VAGUELY
WAN
WISTFUL

Speak Vocabulary Word Search 1 Answer Key

ALLEGEDLY	DEMURE	IMBECILES	RECESSIVE
BANISHED	DENSE	INCITING	REFURBISHED
BIGOTED	DEVIOUS	INCONSPICUOUS	RELUCTANCE
BURROW	DORMANT	INCRIMINATE	SANCTUARY
COAXES	DRONE	INDOCTRINATION	SUBMISSION
CONSCIENCE	DYNAMICS	LEPER	TENACIOUS
CONUNDRUM	ERRANT	MOMENTUM	VAGUELY
DEGRADING	FOSTER	MUSE	WAN
DELINQUENCY	GENETICS	PRUNING	WISTFUL
DEMERit	HAZING	PSEUDO	

Speak Vocabulary Word Search 2

```
D C E S D E L I N Q U E N C Y K J J
Y O R D E T O G I B J W D T J R T C
N N R E C N A T C U L E R H R C Z
A U A G Z C S D C Q P J O K E R R G
M N N F J Q E I I P B S N P W M N G
I D T D E H S I B R U F E R U M E D
C R Y S S N M O I D L M U T N M V
S U D I P T L O H W L Z D T D N Y N
M M N M R P Y M P Z P I E R O T Z
V A G U E L Y Y M E O G N I T I C N I V R
B F E S B U Y N N N I S I A M V Y
F O N E U F G T E X R S U W E X I S
G S E P R T P U X E I N J H S S T Q
Q T T B R S T M M M P Y D C A D C C
J E I H O I J E B L R M A R N O E X
B R C V W W D U N A H Z L T C R J S
N R S S X Z S C I A W F A Z T M B X
D E N S E N T P O G C E M F U A U T
H A Z I N G S N N A R I F J A N S T
S E L I C E B M I P O K R T T Q
S U O I V E D X E H N E R U Y C M H
P R U N I N G R C M K S S S S D F W
```

BANISHED	DENSE	HAZING	PSEUDO	TENACIOUS
BIGOTED	DEVIOUS	IMBECILES	REFURBISHED	VAGUELY
BURROW	DORMANT	INCITING	RELUCTANCE	VESPIARY
COAXES	DRONE	LEPER	RETREAT	WAN
CONUNDRUM	DYNAMICS	MALADJUSTED	SANCTUARY	WISTFUL
DELINQUENCY	ERRANT	MOMENTUM	SENSIBILITIES	XENOPHOBIC
DEMERIT	FOSTER	MUSE	SUBJECTIVITY	
DEMURE	GENETICS	PRUNING	SUBMISSION	

Speak Vocabulary Word Search 2 Answer Key

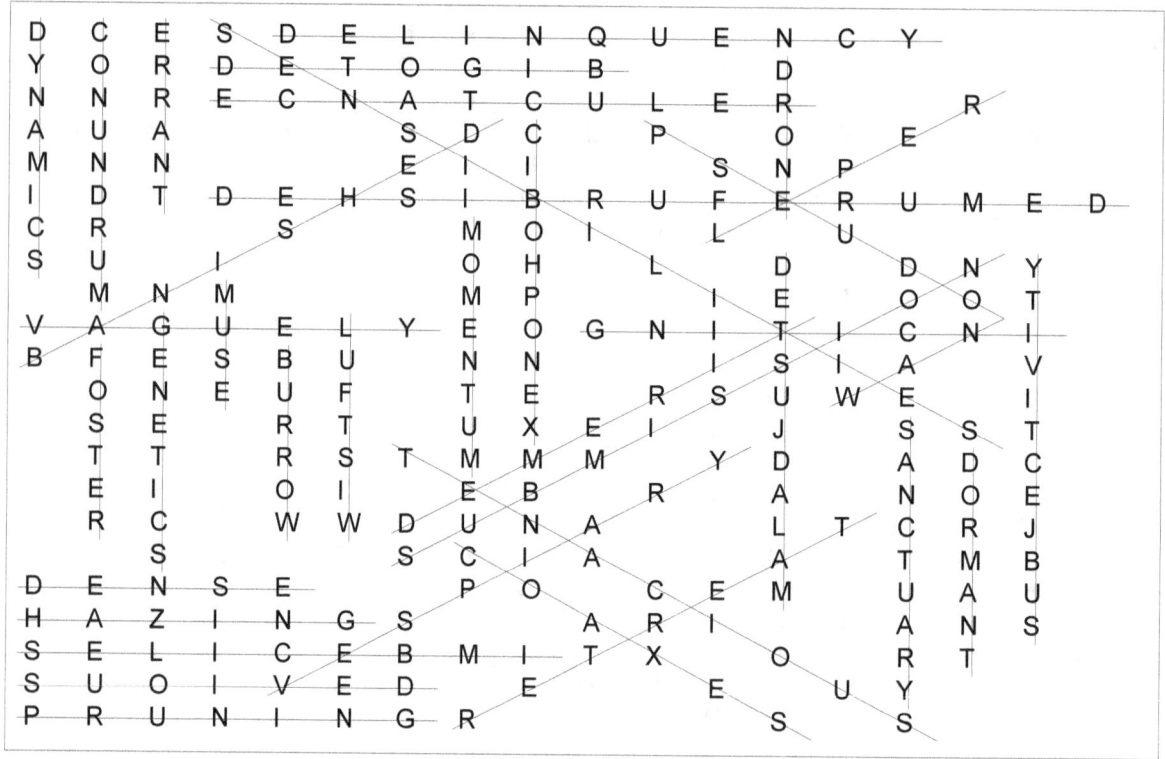

BANISHED	DENSE	HAZING	PSEUDO	TENACIOUS
BIGOTED	DEVIOUS	IMBECILES	REFURBISHED	VAGUELY
BURROW	DORMANT	INCITING	RELUCTANCE	VESPIARY
COAXES	DRONE	LEPER	RETREAT	WAN
CONUNDRUM	DYNAMICS	MALADJUSTED	SANCTUARY	WISTFUL
DELINQUENCY	ERRANT	MOMENTUM	SENSIBILITIES	XENOPHOBIC
DEMERIT	FOSTER	MUSE	SUBJECTIVITY	
DEMURE	GENETICS	PRUNING	SUBMISSION	

Speak Vocabulary Word Search 3

```
B U R R O W D D D G X L Z Q M S L H I
E R R A N T F D E N S E P S E U D O N
R C K Y V K Q N G M T P R Q F O S D C
N O Y K S E E Z R C U E N T R I M E R
F N A W C T S H A T N R S H E V A H I
I S T K I N E P D V N I E A L E L S M
N C Z C M A L H I J W P X Z U D A I I
C I S M A M I D N A D R G A I C F D N
O E D O N R C S G D R G O N T O J A A
N N E M Y O E V U N E Y C G A S U B T
S C L E D D B C A B P M S S N T S S E
P E I N E C M F E G J Q E M C E T U A
I B N T H O I L X S U E V R E R E O L
C I Q U S N N O E U S E C X I N D I L
U G U M I S C U N B D I L T Z T D C E
O O E G B I I N O M D R V Y I G B A G
U T N Q R S T D P I Q E O E Q V L N E
T E C M U T I E H S M T W N Y J I E D
S D Y D F E N R O S L R M T E H X T L
T Q N P E N G I B I R E C L N Y N Z Y
D K N N R C K N I O S A N C T U A R Y
D P D D Y Y L G C N N T P R U N I N G
```

Abusing newcomers with humiliating tricks and ridicule before they become a part of the group (6)
Acting clumsily or in confusion (11)
Based on personal feelings rather than facts (12)
Cutting; clipping (7)
Deceitful; not straightforward (7)
Dull or slow-witted (5)
Failure to fulfill a duty or obligation; something wrongful or illegal (11)
Fake; false; pretend (6)
Force or speed of movement (8)
Forced to leave (8)
Going to the back; a gene that does not produce (9)
Having an unreasonable fear or hatred of foreigners (10)
Hole or hideout animals use to take shelter (6)
Humiliating; disgracing (9)
Inactive; asleep (7)
Inner sense of what is right or wrong (10)
Intolerant of any other beliefs or opinions (7)
Keeping the same behavior, form, pattern, or principles (11)
Made clean, bright, or fresh again (11)
Make someone appear guilty of a crime (11)
Mark against someone for misconduct (7)
Nest of social wasps (8)
Not clear or definite (7)
Not in sync with one's circumstances (11)
Not noticeable (13)
Outcast (5)
Pale in color; sickly-looking (3)
Persistent; stubborn; won't give up (9)
Persuades by pleading or flattery (6)
Remote-controlled mechanism (5)
Sacred place offering refuge or safety (9)
Science of heredity and genes (8)
Shy; modest; coy (6)
Social, intellectual, or physical forces that characterize a system or group (8)
Something or someone that is inspiring to an artist (4)
Something that nourishes or cares for (6)
Stirring up (trouble); egging-on (8)
Straying from the right course (6)
Stupid or silly people (9)
Supposedly; put forth as true but not proven (9)
Surrendering power to another (10)
Thoughtful in a sad way; longing (7)
Unwillingness; resistance (10)
Withdraw; go back (7)

Speak Vocabulary Word Search 3 Answer Key

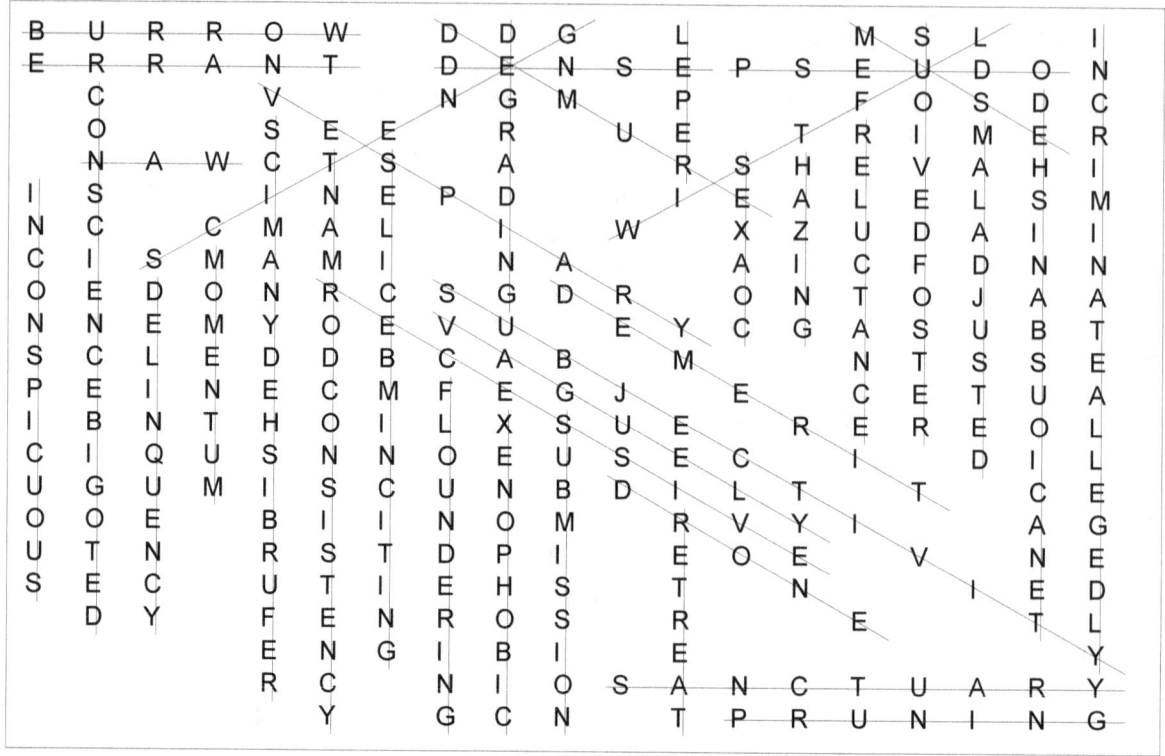

Abusing newcomers with humiliating tricks and ridicule before they become a part of the group (6)
Acting clumsily or in confusion (11)
Based on personal feelings rather than facts (12)
Cutting; clipping (7)
Deceitful; not straightforward (7)
Dull or slow-witted (5)
Failure to fulfill a duty or obligation; something wrongful or illegal (11)
Fake; false; pretend (6)
Force or speed of movement (8)
Forced to leave (8)
Going to the back; a gene that does not produce (9)
Having an unreasonable fear or hatred of foreigners (10)
Hole or hideout animals use to take shelter (6)
Humiliating; disgracing (9)
Inactive; asleep (7)
Inner sense of what is right or wrong (10)
Intolerant of any other beliefs or opinions (7)
Keeping the same behavior, form, pattern, or principles (11)
Made clean, bright, or fresh again (11)
Make someone appear guilty of a crime (11)
Mark against someone for misconduct (7)
Nest of social wasps (8)
Not clear or definite (7)
Not in sync with one's circumstances (11)
Not noticeable (13)
Outcast (5)
Pale in color; sickly-looking (3)
Persistent; stubborn; won't give up (9)
Persuades by pleading or flattery (6)
Remote-controlled mechanism (5)
Sacred place offering refuge or safety (9)
Science of heredity and genes (8)
Shy; modest; coy (6)
Social, intellectual, or physical forces that characterize a system or group (8)
Something or someone that is inspiring to an artist (4)
Something that nourishes or cares for (6)
Stirring up (trouble); egging-on (8)
Straying from the right course (6)
Stupid or silly people (9)
Supposedly; put forth as true but not proven (9)
Surrendering power to another (10)
Thoughtful in a sad way; longing (7)
Unwillingness; resistance (10)
Withdraw; go back (7)

Speak Vocabulary Word Search 4

```
C D S E N S I B I L I T I E S J C S N
B W O R R U B H F J X A N L V V H R O
Q T I R E M E D E S E L I C E B M I I
C Q N A M T R R C B L R B S P R J T
F F C N R A U T N N S E P I P W E L A
Q L I T R M N A T C S G S G I B T R N
L O T D E W T T I O S E E O A F R Z I
D U I D Q C Q T R N B D U T R S E R R
E N N J U O E X T U D L D E Y Y A E T
V D G L E N O R D N W Y O D L X T N C
I E E S E S C S E D B Z N E P S A M O
O R N G T I O U L R D A U A O W X U D
U I W N A S N B I U J G N F M C S S N
S N D I N T S J N M A R G I H I M E I
M G E Z I E C E Q V E V I S S E C E R
O R G A M N I C U K P Q P W Z H P S L
M L R H I C E T E N A C I O U S E P U
E G A H R Y N I N M C C Y Z E W K D F
N P D S C Y C V C Q C Q T X K V F K T
T M I L N D E I Y W Y R A U T C N A S
U Q N J I P F T X E N O P H O B I C I
M X G G H Y G Y T S C P R U N I N G W
```

Abusing newcomers with humiliating tricks and ridicule before they become a part of the group (6)
Acting clumsily or in confusion (11)
Based on personal feelings rather than facts (12)
Cutting; clipping (7)
Deceitful; not straightforward (7)
Difficult problem; dilemma (9)
Dull or slow-witted (5)
Emotions; feelings (13)
Failure to fulfill a duty or obligation; something wrongful or illegal (11)
Fake; false; pretend (6)
Force or speed of movement (8)
Forced to leave (8)
Going to the back; a gene that does not produce (9)
Having an unreasonable fear or hatred of foreigners (10)
Hole or hideout animals use to take shelter (6)
Humiliating; disgracing (9)
Inactive; asleep (7)
Inner sense of what is right or wrong (10)
Intolerant of any other beliefs or opinions (7)
Keeping the same behavior, form, pattern, or principles (11)
Make someone appear guilty of a crime (11)
Mark against someone for misconduct (7)
Nest of social wasps (8)
Not clear or definite (7)
Outcast (5)
Pale in color; sickly-looking (3)
Persistent; stubborn; won't give up (9)
Persuades by pleading or flattery (6)
Remote-controlled mechanism (5)
Sacred place offering refuge or safety (9)
Science of heredity and genes (8)
Shy; modest; coy (6)
Social, intellectual, or physical forces that characterize a system or group (8)
Something or someone that is inspiring to an artist (4)
Something that nourishes or cares for (6)
Stirring up (trouble); egging-on (8)
Straying from the right course (6)
Stupid or silly people (9)
Supposedly; put forth as true but not proven (9)
Teaching someone to accept an idea or principle without criticism (14)
Thoughtful in a sad way; longing (7)
Unwillingness; resistance (10)
Withdraw; go back (7)

Speak Vocabulary Word Search 4 Answer Key

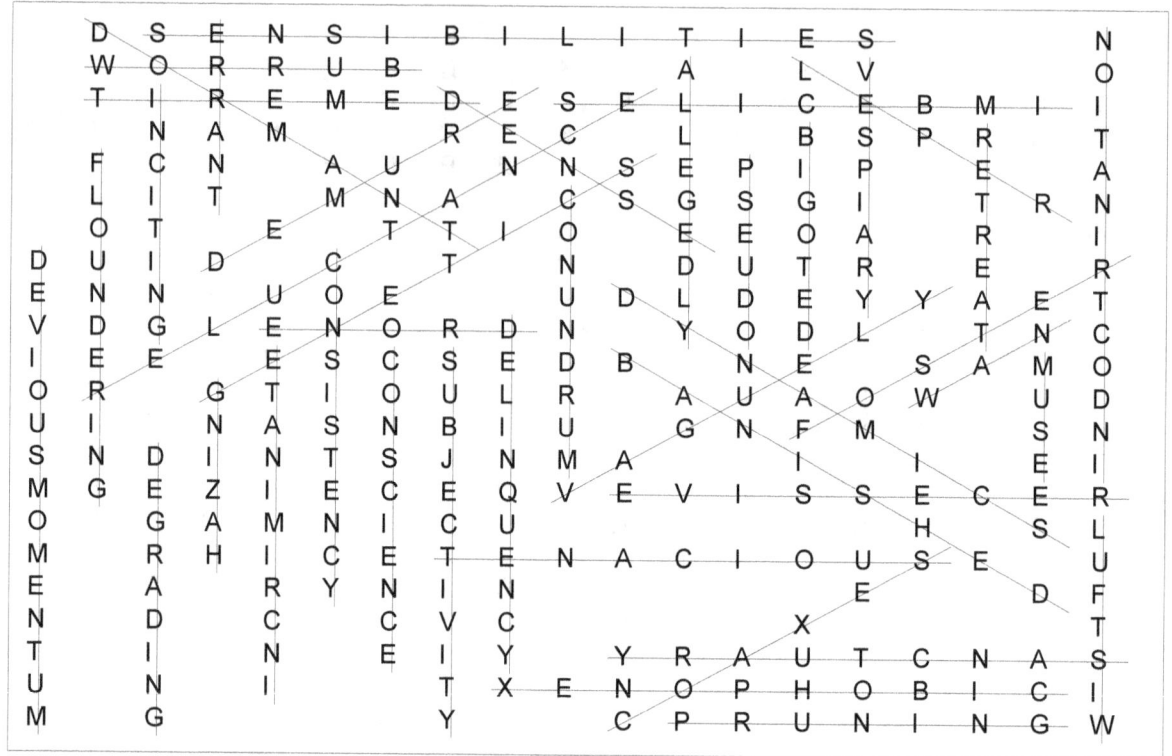

Abusing newcomers with humiliating tricks and ridicule before they become a part of the group (6)
Acting clumsily or in confusion (11)
Based on personal feelings rather than facts (12)
Cutting; clipping (7)
Deceitful; not straightforward (7)
Difficult problem; dilemma (9)
Dull or slow-witted (5)
Emotions; feelings (13)
Failure to fulfill a duty or obligation; something wrongful or illegal (11)
Fake; false; pretend (6)
Force or speed of movement (8)
Forced to leave (8)
Going to the back; a gene that does not produce (9)
Having an unreasonable fear or hatred of foreigners (10)
Hole or hideout animals use to take shelter (6)
Humiliating; disgracing (9)
Inactive; asleep (7)
Inner sense of what is right or wrong (10)
Intolerant of any other beliefs or opinions (7)
Keeping the same behavior, form, pattern, or principles (11)
Make someone appear guilty of a crime (11)
Mark against someone for misconduct (7)
Nest of social wasps (8)
Not clear or definite (7)
Outcast (5)
Pale in color; sickly-looking (3)
Persistent; stubborn; won't give up (9)
Persuades by pleading or flattery (6)
Remote-controlled mechanism (5)
Sacred place offering refuge or safety (9)
Science of heredity and genes (8)
Shy; modest; coy (6)
Social, intellectual, or physical forces that characterize a system or group (8)
Something or someone that is inspiring to an artist (4)
Something that nourishes or cares for (6)
Stirring up (trouble); egging-on (8)
Straying from the right course (6)
Stupid or silly people (9)
Supposedly; put forth as true but not proven (9)
Teaching someone to accept an idea or principle without criticism (14)
Thoughtful in a sad way; longing (7)
Unwillingness; resistance (10)
Withdraw; go back (7)

Speak Vocabulary Crossword 1

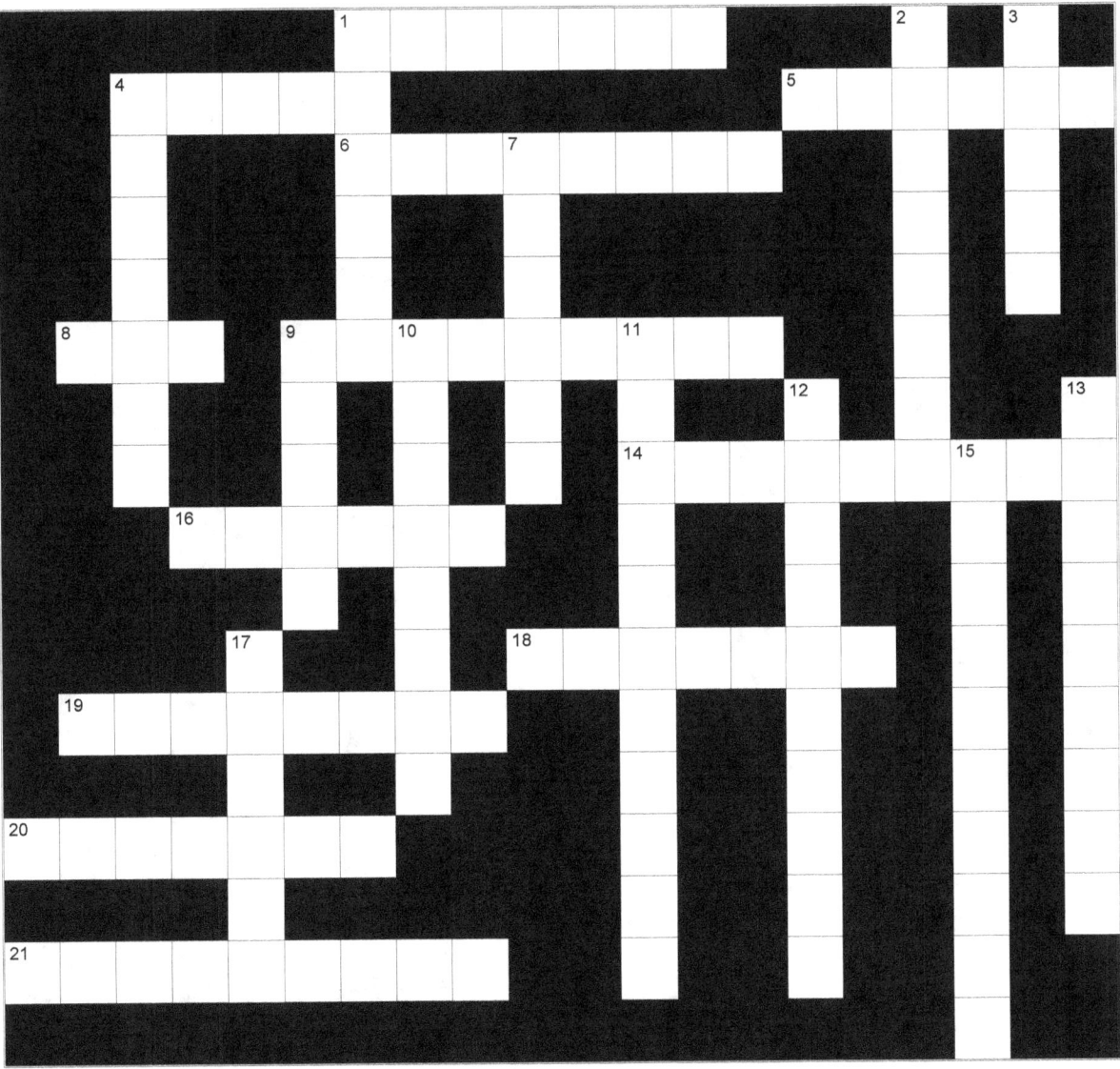

Across
1. Deceitful; not straightforward
4. Remote-controlled mechanism
5. Persuades by pleading or flattery
6. Force or speed of movement
8. Pale in color; sickly-looking
9. Humiliating; disgracing
14. Difficult problem; dilemma
16. Something that nourishes or cares for
18. Mark against someone for misconduct
19. Social, intellectual, or physical forces that characterize a system or group
20. Cutting; clipping
21. Supposedly; put forth as true but not proven

Down
1. Shy; modest; coy
2. Forced to leave
3. Outcast
4. Inactive; asleep
7. Straying from the right course
9. Dull or slow-witted
10. Science of heredity and genes
11. Make someone appear guilty of a crime
12. Surrendering power to another
13. Stupid or silly people
15. How the public views or regards an individual
17. Abusing newcomers with humiliating tricks and ridicule before they become a part of the group

Speak Vocabulary Crossword 1 Answer Key

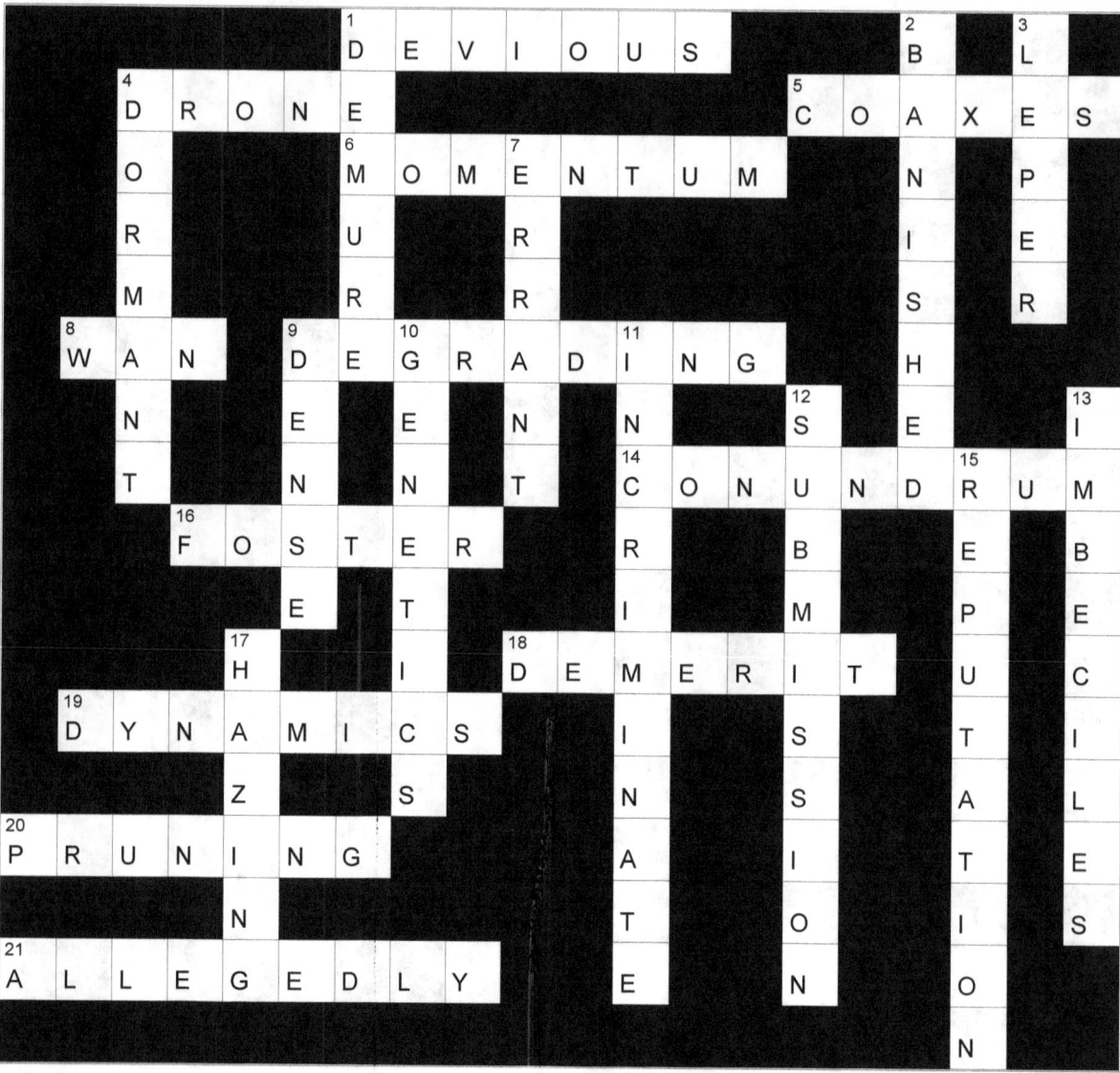

Across
1. Deceitful; not straightforward
4. Remote-controlled mechanism
5. Persuades by pleading or flattery
6. Force or speed of movement
8. Pale in color; sickly-looking
9. Humiliating; disgracing
14. Difficult problem; dilemma
16. Something that nourishes or cares for
18. Mark against someone for misconduct
19. Social, intellectual, or physical forces that characterize a system or group
20. Cutting; clipping
21. Supposedly; put forth as true but not proven

Down
1. Shy; modest; coy
2. Forced to leave
3. Outcast
4. Inactive; asleep
7. Straying from the right course
9. Dull or slow-witted
10. Science of heredity and genes
11. Make someone appear guilty of a crime
12. Surrendering power to another
13. Stupid or silly people
15. How the public views or regards an individual
17. Abusing newcomers with humiliating tricks and ridicule before they become a part of the group

Speak Vocabulary Crossword 2

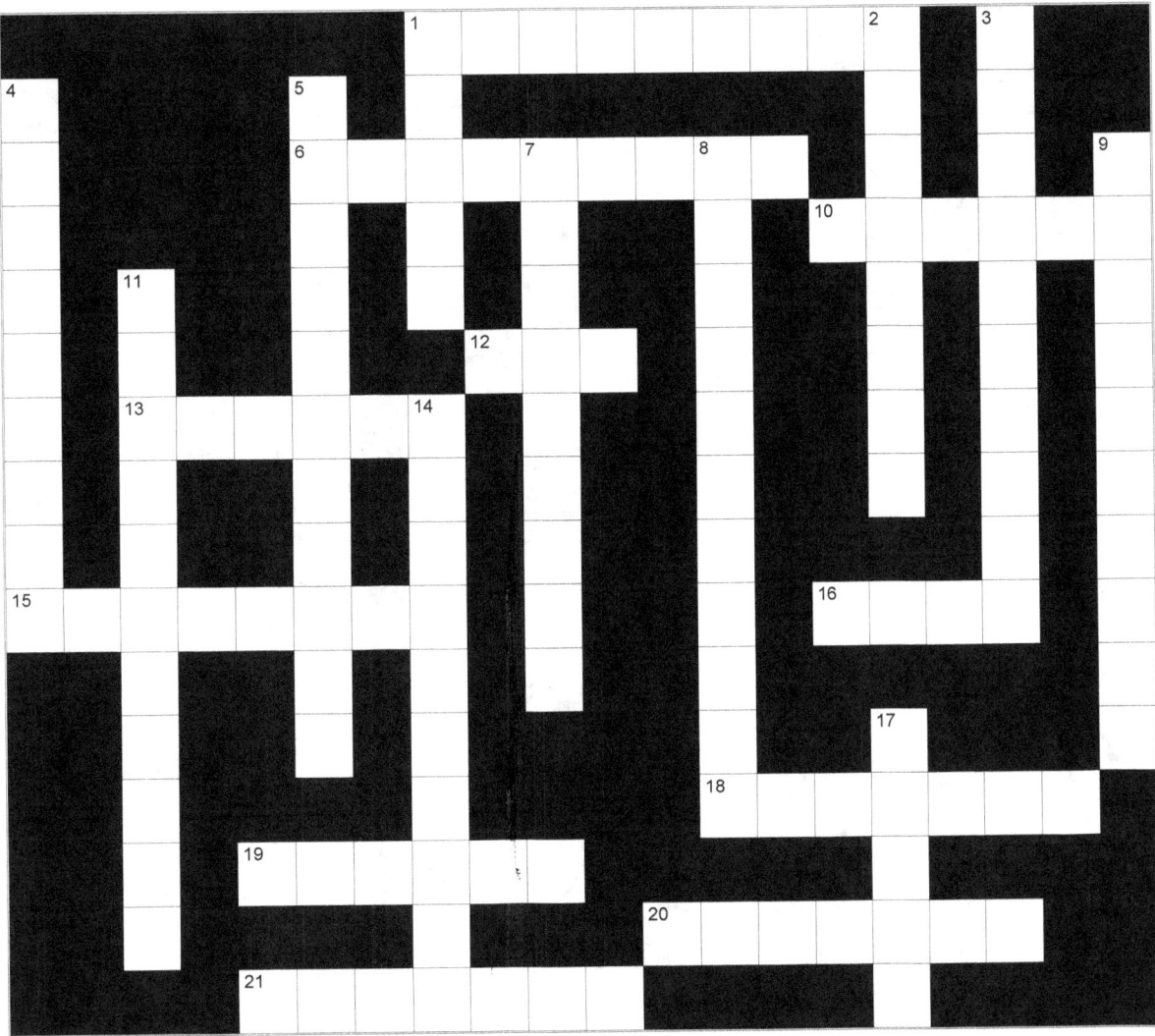

Across
1. Humiliating; disgracing
6. Sacred place offering refuge or safety
10. Shy; modest; coy
12. Pale in color; sickly-looking
13. Persuades by pleading or flattery
15. Force or speed of movement
16. Something or someone that is inspiring to an artist
18. Mark against someone for misconduct
19. Abusing newcomers with humiliating tricks and ridicule before they become a part of the group
20. Not clear or definite
21. Cutting; clipping

Down
1. Dull or slow-witted
2. Science of heredity and genes
3. Unwillingness; resistance
4. Difficult problem; dilemma
5. Suffocated; smothered; choked
7. Persistent; stubborn; won't give up
8. Made clean, bright, or fresh again
9. Having an unreasonable fear or hatred of foreigners
11. Make someone appear guilty of a crime
14. Surrendering power to another
17. Outcast

Speak Vocabulary Crossword 2 Answer Key

Across
1. Humiliating; disgracing
6. Sacred place offering refuge or safety
10. Shy; modest; coy
12. Pale in color; sickly-looking
13. Persuades by pleading or flattery
15. Force or speed of movement
16. Something or someone that is inspiring to an artist
18. Mark against someone for misconduct
19. Abusing newcomers with humiliating tricks and ridicule before they become a part of the group
20. Not clear or definite
21. Cutting; clipping

Down
1. Dull or slow-witted
2. Science of heredity and genes
3. Unwillingness; resistance
4. Difficult problem; dilemma
5. Suffocated; smothered; choked
7. Persistent; stubborn; won't give up
8. Made clean, bright, or fresh again
9. Having an unreasonable fear or hatred of foreigners
11. Make someone appear guilty of a crime
14. Surrendering power to another
17. Outcast

Speak Vocabulary Crossword 3

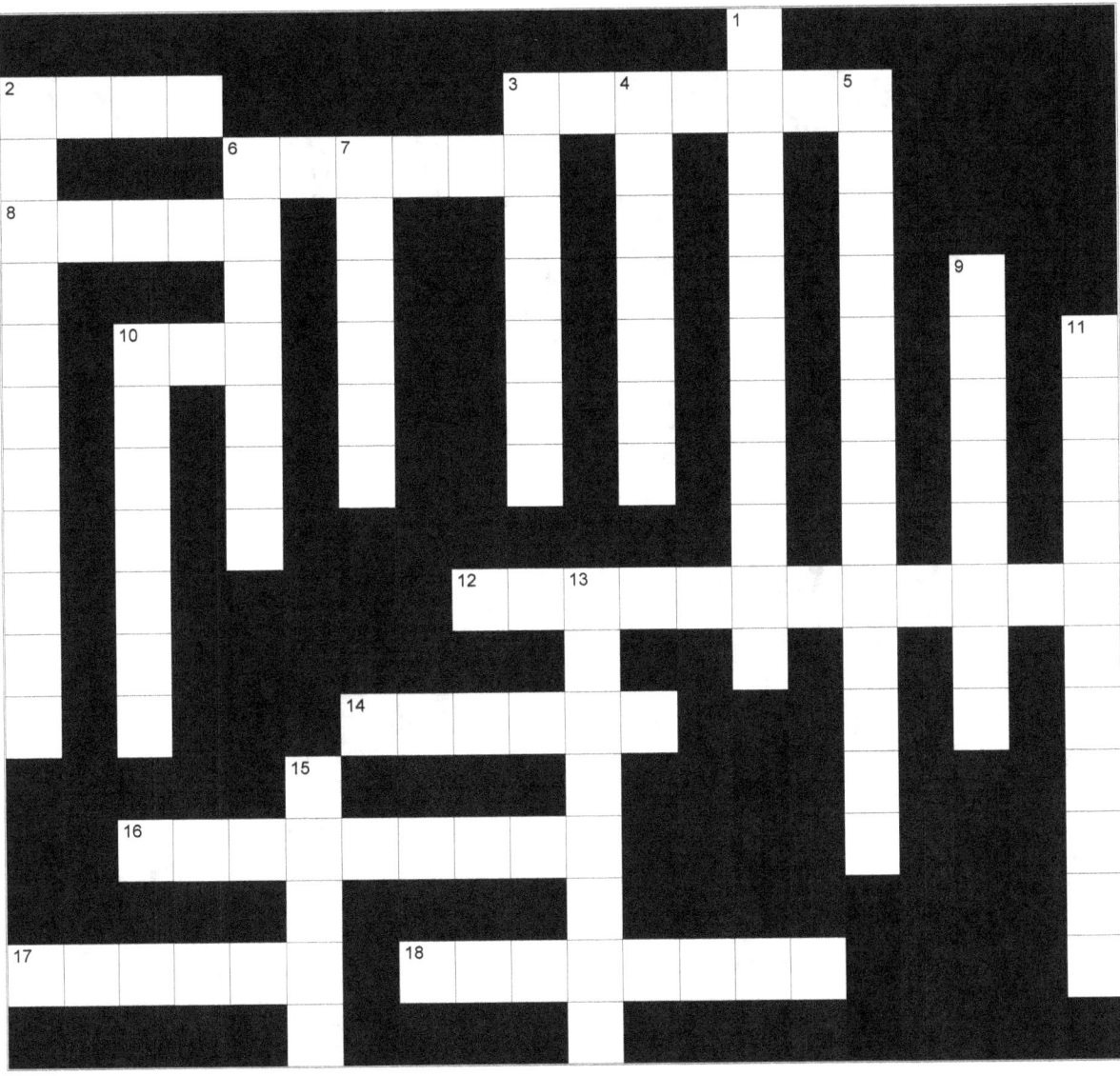

Across
2. Something or someone that is inspiring to an artist
3. Deceitful; not straightforward
6. Fake; false; pretend
8. Outcast
10. Pale in color; sickly-looking
12. Based on personal feelings rather than facts
14. Abusing newcomers with humiliating tricks and ridicule before they become a part of the group
16. Stupid or silly people
17. Persuades by pleading or flattery
18. Science of heredity and genes

Down
1. Keeping the same behavior, form, pattern, or principles
2. Not in sync with one's circumstances
3. Inactive; asleep
4. Not clear or definite
5. Emotions; feelings
6. Cutting; clipping
7. Straying from the right course
9. Stirring up (trouble); egging-on
10. Thoughtful in a sad way; longing
11. Suffocated; smothered; choked
13. Forced to leave
15. Dull or slow-witted

Speak Vocabulary Crossword 3 Answer Key

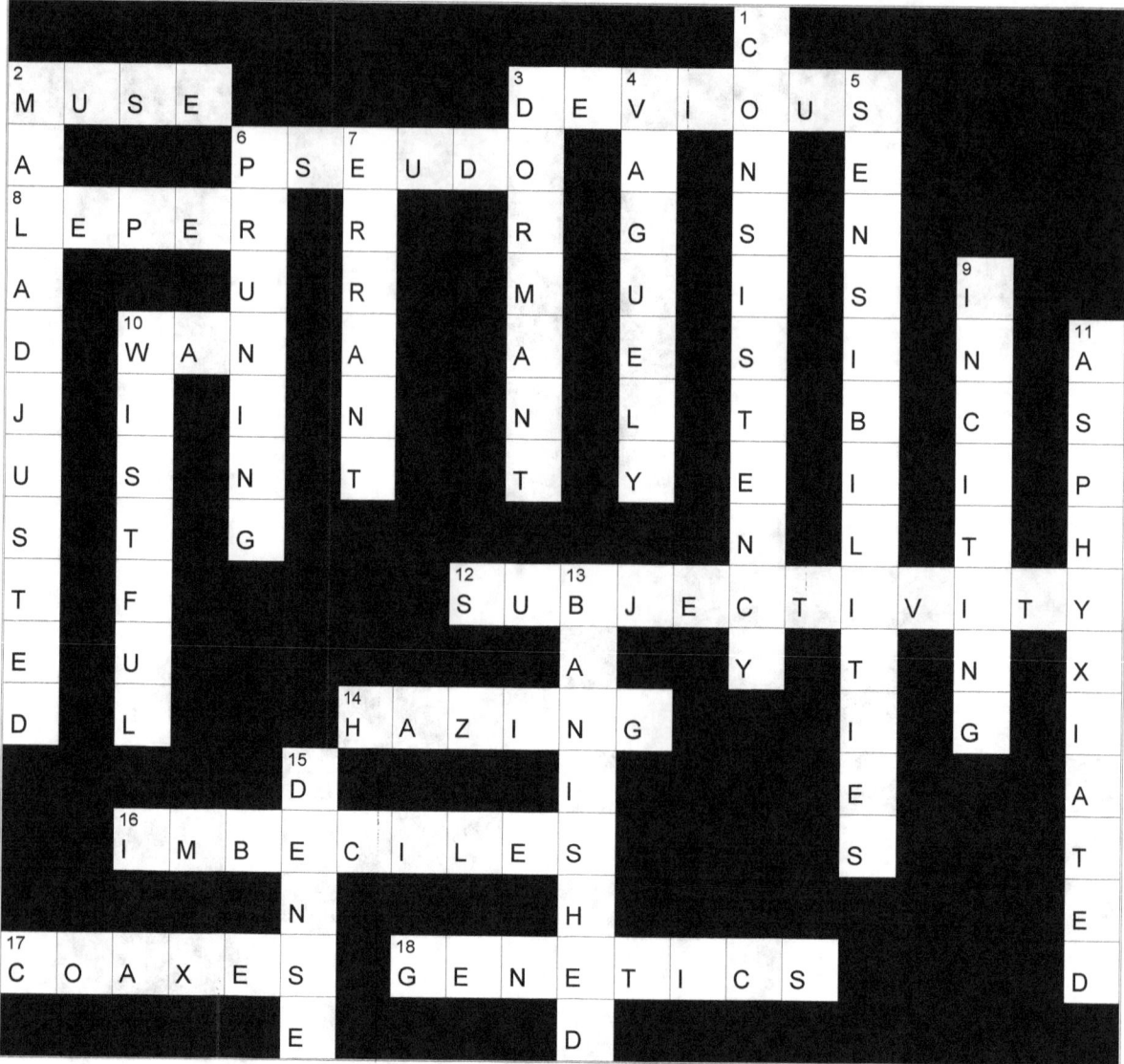

Across
2. Something or someone that is inspiring to an artist
3. Deceitful; not straightforward
6. Fake; false; pretend
8. Outcast
10. Pale in color; sickly-looking
12. Based on personal feelings rather than facts
14. Abusing newcomers with humiliating tricks and ridicule before they become a part of the group
16. Stupid or silly people
17. Persuades by pleading or flattery
18. Science of heredity and genes

Down
1. Keeping the same behavior, form, pattern, or principles
2. Not in sync with one's circumstances
3. Inactive; asleep
4. Not clear or definite
5. Emotions; feelings
6. Cutting; clipping
7. Straying from the right course
9. Stirring up (trouble); egging-on
10. Thoughtful in a sad way; longing
11. Suffocated; smothered; choked
13. Forced to leave
15. Dull or slow-witted

Speak Vocabulary Crossword 4

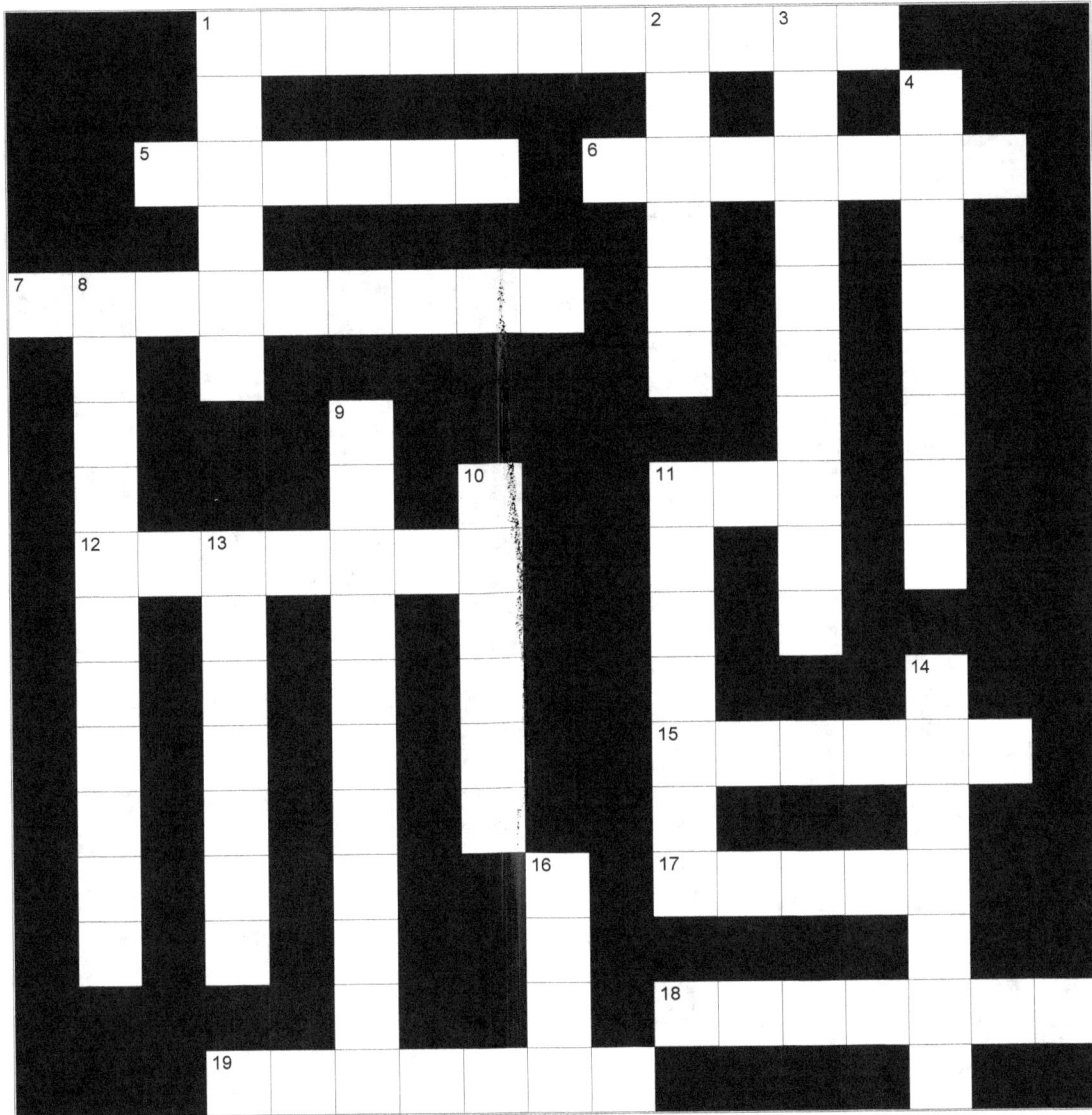

Across
1. Keeping the same behavior, form, pattern, or principles
5. Abusing newcomers with humiliating tricks and ridicule before they become a part of the group
6. Cutting; clipping
7. Stupid or silly people
11. Pale in color; sickly-looking
12. Deceitful; not straightforward
15. Something that nourishes or cares for
17. Outcast
18. Inactive; asleep
19. Intolerant of any other beliefs or opinions

Down
1. Persuades by pleading or flattery
2. Straying from the right course
3. Inner sense of what is right or wrong
4. Stirring up (trouble); egging-on
8. Not in sync with one's circumstances
9. Acting clumsily or in confusion
10. Fake; false; pretend
11. Thoughtful in a sad way; longing
13. Not clear or definite
14. Withdraw; go back
16. Something or someone that is inspiring to an artist

Speak Vocabulary Crossword 4 Answer Key

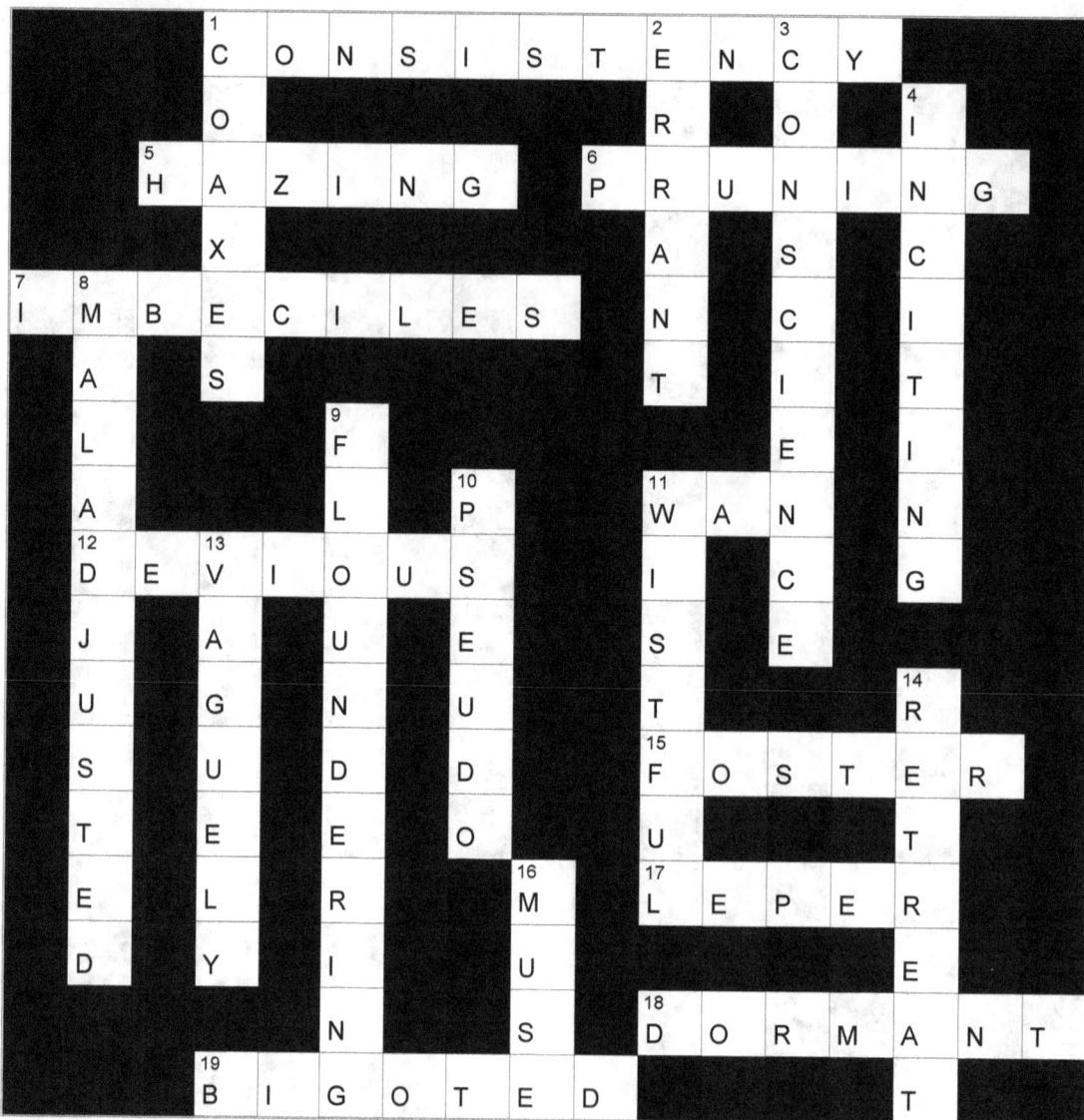

Across
1. Keeping the same behavior, form, pattern, or principles
5. Abusing newcomers with humiliating tricks and ridicule before they become a part of the group
6. Cutting; clipping
7. Stupid or silly people
11. Pale in color; sickly-looking
12. Deceitful; not straightforward
15. Something that nourishes or cares for
17. Outcast
18. Inactive; asleep
19. Intolerant of any other beliefs or opinions

Down
1. Persuades by pleading or flattery
2. Straying from the right course
3. Inner sense of what is right or wrong
4. Stirring up (trouble); egging-on
8. Not in sync with one's circumstances
9. Acting clumsily or in confusion
10. Fake; false; pretend
11. Thoughtful in a sad way; longing
13. Not clear or definite
14. Withdraw; go back
16. Something or someone that is inspiring to an artist

Speak Vocabulary Juggle Letters 1

1. CNQEILEUYND = 1. _____
   Failure to fulfill a duty or obligation; something wrongful or illegal

2. IUBSMNSIOS = 2. _____
   Surrendering power to another

3. USEDOP = 3. _____
   Fake; false; pretend

4. CINGITIN = 4. _____
   Stirring up (trouble); egging-on

5. EEPLR = 5. _____
   Outcast

6. SCEONCCNEI = 6. _____
   Inner sense of what is right or wrong

7. NEORD = 7. _____
   Remote-controlled mechanism

8. EILBCIEMS = 8. _____
   Stupid or silly people

9. NOIEARTPUT = 9. _____
   How the public views or regards an individual

10. CIOXOHBEPN =10. _____
    Having an unreasonable fear or hatred of foreigners

11. URONAVYLITOER =11. _____
    Supporting radical change or innovation

12. AGRDGEDIN =12. _____
    Humiliating; disgracing

13. TOMDRAN =13. _____
    Inactive; asleep

14. GHNAZI =14. _____
    Abusing newcomers with humiliating tricks and ridicule before they become a part of the group

15. ANW =15. _____
    Pale in color; sickly-looking

Speak Vocabulary Juggle Letters 1 Answer Key

1. CNQEILEUYND = 1. DELINQUENCY
Failure to fulfill a duty or obligation; something wrongful or illegal

2. IUBSMNSIOS = 2. SUBMISSION
Surrendering power to another

3. USEDOP = 3. PSEUDO
Fake; false; pretend

4. CINGITIN = 4. INCITING
Stirring up (trouble); egging-on

5. EEPLR = 5. LEPER
Outcast

6. SCEONCCNEI = 6. CONSCIENCE
Inner sense of what is right or wrong

7. NEORD = 7. DRONE
Remote-controlled mechanism

8. EILBCIEMS = 8. IMBECILES
Stupid or silly people

9. NOIEARTPUT = 9. REPUTATION
How the public views or regards an individual

10. CIOXOHBEPN = 10. XENOPHOBIC
Having an unreasonable fear or hatred of foreigners

11. URONAVYLITOER = 11. REVOLUTIONARY
Supporting radical change or innovation

12. AGRDGEDIN = 12. DEGRADING
Humiliating; disgracing

13. TOMDRAN = 13. DORMANT
Inactive; asleep

14. GHNAZI = 14. HAZING
Abusing newcomers with humiliating tricks and ridicule before they become a part of the group

15. ANW = 15. WAN
Pale in color; sickly-looking

Speak Vocabulary Juggle Letters 2

1. EUYALGV = 1. _____
Not clear or definite

2. USNOOICCNUISP = 2. _____
Not noticeable

3. OSANTCIUE = 3. _____
Persistent; stubborn; won't give up

4. ODNTARM = 4. _____
Inactive; asleep

5. GERGNIADD = 5. _____
Humiliating; disgracing

6. EAIORNTTPU = 6. _____
How the public views or regards an individual

7. NSCCICONEE = 7. _____
Inner sense of what is right or wrong

8. UESPDO = 8. _____
Fake; false; pretend

9. INAZHG = 9. _____
Abusing newcomers with humiliating tricks and ridicule before they become a part of the group

10. UDEEMR = 10. _____
Shy; modest; coy

11. TNCGIIIN = 11. _____
Stirring up (trouble); egging-on

12. NWA = 12. _____
Pale in color; sickly-looking

13. LLLEGDAEY = 13. _____
Supposedly; put forth as true but not proven

14. GINOUDFLNRE = 14. _____
Acting clumsily or in confusion

15. TERARN = 15. _____
Straying from the right course

Speak Vocabulary Juggle Letters 2 Answer Key

1. EUYALGV = 1. VAGUELY
   Not clear or definite

2. USNOOICCNUISP = 2. INCONSPICUOUS
   Not noticeable

3. OSANTCIUE = 3. TENACIOUS
   Persistent; stubborn; won't give up

4. ODNTARM = 4. DORMANT
   Inactive; asleep

5. GERGNIADD = 5. DEGRADING
   Humiliating; disgracing

6. EAIORNTTPU = 6. REPUTATION
   How the public views or regards an individual

7. NSCCICONEE = 7. CONSCIENCE
   Inner sense of what is right or wrong

8. UESPDO = 8. PSEUDO
   Fake; false; pretend

9. INAZHG = 9. HAZING
   Abusing newcomers with humiliating tricks and ridicule before they become a part of the group

10. UDEEMR =10. DEMURE
    Shy; modest; coy

11. TNCGIIIN =11. INCITING
    Stirring up (trouble); egging-on

12. NWA =12. WAN
    Pale in color; sickly-looking

13. LLLEGDAEY =13. ALLEGEDLY
    Supposedly; put forth as true but not proven

14. GINOUDFLNRE =14. FLOUNDERING
    Acting clumsily or in confusion

15. TERARN =15. ERRANT
    Straying from the right course

Speak Vocabulary Juggle Letters 3

1. AERTTER = 1. _____
   Withdraw; go back

2. DELALEGYL = 2. _____
   Supposedly; put forth as true but not proven

3. OINETARPTU = 3. _____
   How the public views or regards an individual

4. EUYGAVL = 4. _____
   Not clear or definite

5. SLUTIWF = 5. _____
   Thoughtful in a sad way; longing

6. CESNTYOCNIS = 6. _____
   Keeping the same behavior, form, pattern, or principles

7. OEOBCPIXHN = 7. _____
   Having an unreasonable fear or hatred of foreigners

8. IBTEJSTCIUYV = 8. _____
   Based on personal feelings rather than facts

9. EMEDTRI = 9. _____
   Mark against someone for misconduct

10. OIDTEBG = 10. _____
    Intolerant of any other beliefs or opinions

11. WAN = 11. _____
    Pale in color; sickly-looking

12. NDREO = 12. _____
    Remote-controlled mechanism

13. GNHAIZ = 13. _____
    Abusing newcomers with humiliating tricks and ridicule before they become a part of the group

14. YSTCRUNAA = 14. _____
    Sacred place offering refuge or safety

15. JLDSDUTEAAM = 15. _____
    Not in sync with one's circumstances

Speak Vocabulary Juggle Letters 3 Answer Key

1. AERTTER = 1. RETREAT
Withdraw; go back

2. DELALEGYL = 2. ALLEGEDLY
Supposedly; put forth as true but not proven

3. OINETARPTU = 3. REPUTATION
How the public views or regards an individual

4. EUYGAVL = 4. VAGUELY
Not clear or definite

5. SLUTIWF = 5. WISTFUL
Thoughtful in a sad way; longing

6. CESNTYOCNIS = 6. CONSISTENCY
Keeping the same behavior, form, pattern, or principles

7. OEOBCPIXHN = 7. XENOPHOBIC
Having an unreasonable fear or hatred of foreigners

8. IBTEJSTCIUYV = 8. SUBJECTIVITY
Based on personal feelings rather than facts

9. EMEDTRI = 9. DEMERIT
Mark against someone for misconduct

10. OIDTEBG = 10. BIGOTED
Intolerant of any other beliefs or opinions

11. WAN = 11. WAN
Pale in color; sickly-looking

12. NDREO = 12. DRONE
Remote-controlled mechanism

13. GNHAIZ = 13. HAZING
Abusing newcomers with humiliating tricks and ridicule before they become a part of the group

14. YSTCRUNAA = 14. SANCTUARY
Sacred place offering refuge or safety

15. JLDSDUTEAAM = 15. MALADJUSTED
Not in sync with one's circumstances

Speak Vocabulary Juggle Letters 4

1. ESUM = 1. _____
Something or someone that is inspiring to an artist

2. NEDOR = 2. _____
Remote-controlled mechanism

3. EUOSDVI = 3. _____
Deceitful; not straightforward

4. OCNCIESENC = 4. _____
Inner sense of what is right or wrong

5. SCECITYSNNO = 5. _____
Keeping the same behavior, form, pattern, or principles

6. NIRGNUP = 6. _____
Cutting; clipping

7. MEDTREI = 7. _____
Mark against someone for misconduct

8. DADASTLMUEJ = 8. _____
Not in sync with one's circumstances

9. XSAOEC = 9. _____
Persuades by pleading or flattery

10. RONDTMA =10. _____
Inactive; asleep

11. RWBORU =11. _____
Hole or hideout animals use to take shelter

12. SILIEINSEITSB =12. _____
Emotions; feelings

13. UMDREE =13. _____
Shy; modest; coy

14. NMYSCAID =14. _____
Social, intellectual, or physical forces that characterize a system or group

15. ICNNGTII =15. _____
Stirring up (trouble); egging-on

Speak Vocabulary Juggle Letters 4 Answer Key

1. ESUM = 1. MUSE
Something or someone that is inspiring to an artist

2. NEDOR = 2. DRONE
Remote-controlled mechanism

3. EUOSDVI = 3. DEVIOUS
Deceitful; not straightforward

4. OCNCIESENC = 4. CONSCIENCE
Inner sense of what is right or wrong

5. SCECITYSNNO = 5. CONSISTENCY
Keeping the same behavior, form, pattern, or principles

6. NIRGNUP = 6. PRUNING
Cutting; clipping

7. MEDTREI = 7. DEMERIT
Mark against someone for misconduct

8. DADASTLMUEJ = 8. MALADJUSTED
Not in sync with one's circumstances

9. XSAOEC = 9. COAXES
Persuades by pleading or flattery

10. RONDTMA = 10. DORMANT
Inactive; asleep

11. RWBORU = 11. BURROW
Hole or hideout animals use to take shelter

12. SILIEINSEITSB = 12. SENSIBILITIES
Emotions; feelings

13. UMDREE = 13. DEMURE
Shy; modest; coy

14. NMYSCAID = 14. DYNAMICS
Social, intellectual, or physical forces that characterize a system or group

15. ICNNGTII = 15. INCITING
Stirring up (trouble); egging-on

ALLEGEDLY	Supposedly; put forth as true but not proven
ASPHYXIATED	Suffocated; smothered; choked
BANISHED	Forced to leave
BIGOTED	Intolerant of any other beliefs or opinions
BURROW	Hole or hideout animals use to take shelter

COAXES	Persuades by pleading or flattery
CONSCIENCE	Inner sense of what is right or wrong
CONSISTENCY	Keeping the same behavior, form, pattern, or principles
CONUNDRUM	Difficult problem; dilemma
DEGRADING	Humiliating; disgracing

DELINQUENCY	Failure to fulfill a duty or obligation; something wrongful or illegal
DEMERIT	Mark against someone for misconduct
DEMURE	Shy; modest; coy
DENSE	Dull or slow-witted
DEVIOUS	Deceitful; not straightforward

DORMANT	Inactive; asleep
DRONE	Remote-controlled mechanism
DYNAMICS	Social, intellectual, or physical forces that characterize a system or group
ERRANT	Straying from the right course
FLOUNDERING	Acting clumsily or in confusion

FOSTER	Something that nourishes or cares for
GENETICS	Science of heredity and genes
HAZING	Abusing newcomers with humiliating tricks and ridicule before they become a part of the group
IMBECILES	Stupid or silly people
INCITING	Stirring up (trouble); egging-on

INCONSPICUOUS	Not noticeable
INCRIMINATE	Make someone appear guilty of a crime
INDOCTRINATION	Teaching someone to accept an idea or principle without criticism
LEPER	Outcast
MALADJUSTED	Not in sync with one's circumstances

MOMENTUM	Force or speed of movement
MUSE	Something or someone that is inspiring to an artist
PRUNING	Cutting; clipping
PSEUDO	Fake; false; pretend
RECESSIVE	Going to the back; a gene that does not produce

REFURBISHED	Made clean, bright, or fresh again
RELUCTANCE	Unwillingness; resistance
REPUTATION	How the public views or regards an individual
RETREAT	Withdraw; go back
REVOLUTIONARY	Supporting radical change or innovation

SANCTUARY	Sacred place offering refuge or safety
SENSIBILITIES	Emotions; feelings
SUBJECTIVITY	Based on personal feelings rather than facts
SUBMISSION	Surrendering power to another
TENACIOUS	Persistent; stubborn; won't give up

VAGUELY	Not clear or definite
VESPIARY	Nest of social wasps
WAN	Pale in color; sickly-looking
WISTFUL	Thoughtful in a sad way; longing
XENOPHOBIC	Having an unreasonable fear or hatred of foreigners

Speak Vocabulary

DEMERIT	MALADJUSTED	SANCTUARY	INCONSPICUOUS	INCITING
SUBMISSION	DENSE	FOSTER	ASPHYXIATED	DRONE
PSEUDO	SENSIBILITIES	FREE SPACE	COAXES	PRUNING
CONSISTENCY	HAZING	DEMURE	RECESSIVE	LEPER
RETREAT	REPUTATION	BURROW	CONUNDRUM	FLOUNDERING

Speak Vocabulary

BIGOTED	ERRANT	DEVIOUS	MUSE	VAGUELY
IMBECILES	DEGRADING	VESPIARY	REVOLUTIONARY	CONSCIENCE
MOMENTUM	XENOPHOBIC	FREE SPACE	INCRIMINATE	ALLEGEDLY
REFURBISHED	DELINQUENCY	BANISHED	DORMANT	RELUCTANCE
DYNAMICS	GENETICS	INDOCTRINATION	WAN	WISTFUL

Speak Vocabulary

DELINQUENCY	DYNAMICS	RELUCTANCE	DEMERIT	DEVIOUS
SUBMISSION	XENOPHOBIC	DENSE	DEGRADING	HAZING
MALADJUSTED	SANCTUARY	FREE SPACE	ASPHYXIATED	REPUTATION
MOMENTUM	INCRIMINATE	REVOLUTIONARY	PSEUDO	CONSCIENCE
SUBJECTIVITY	RECESSIVE	SENSIBILITIES	CONSISTENCY	FLOUNDERING

Speak Vocabulary

VESPIARY	INDOCTRINATION	MUSE	INCONSPICUOUS	DORMANT
BIGOTED	LEPER	IMBECILES	WAN	RETREAT
ERRANT	ALLEGEDLY	FREE SPACE	REFURBISHED	DEMURE
COAXES	INCITING	VAGUELY	TENACIOUS	GENETICS
WISTFUL	CONUNDRUM	PRUNING	BURROW	FOSTER

Speak Vocabulary

RECESSIVE	VAGUELY	FLOUNDERING	DYNAMICS	MOMENTUM
DEGRADING	RELUCTANCE	CONSCIENCE	REVOLUTIONARY	ALLEGEDLY
REPUTATION	VESPIARY	FREE SPACE	MUSE	FOSTER
INCITING	PRUNING	ERRANT	HAZING	TENACIOUS
XENOPHOBIC	INCRIMINATE	WAN	BURROW	INCONSPICUOUS

Speak Vocabulary

BIGOTED	LEPER	PSEUDO	DORMANT	DEMERIT
REFURBISHED	RETREAT	INDOCTRINATION	CONUNDRUM	COAXES
DELINQUENCY	SUBMISSION	FREE SPACE	SENSIBILITIES	ASPHYXIATED
SUBJECTIVITY	SANCTUARY	GENETICS	WISTFUL	IMBECILES
BANISHED	DENSE	DRONE	MALADJUSTED	CONSISTENCY

Speak Vocabulary

PSEUDO	WAN	MUSE	CONSCIENCE	REVOLUTIONARY
CONSISTENCY	FOSTER	ERRANT	TENACIOUS	DEGRADING
VESPIARY	VAGUELY	FREE SPACE	RELUCTANCE	HAZING
SANCTUARY	INDOCTRINATION	INCRIMINATE	SUBMISSION	REPUTATION
REFURBISHED	RECESSIVE	INCITING	IMBECILES	BURROW

Speak Vocabulary

DEVIOUS	BIGOTED	MOMENTUM	ASPHYXIATED	ALLEGEDLY
DENSE	DYNAMICS	DORMANT	WISTFUL	BANISHED
LEPER	FLOUNDERING	FREE SPACE	RETREAT	SENSIBILITIES
GENETICS	DELINQUENCY	PRUNING	MALADJUSTED	COAXES
DEMERIT	SUBJECTIVITY	XENOPHOBIC	DRONE	CONUNDRUM

Speak Vocabulary

RELUCTANCE	REVOLUTIONARY	ERRANT	DEMERIT	CONUNDRUM
SUBMISSION	BANISHED	ASPHYXIATED	TENACIOUS	INDOCTRINATION
DEVIOUS	GENETICS	FREE SPACE	FOSTER	CONSCIENCE
INCONSPICUOUS	DEGRADING	DENSE	IMBECILES	MOMENTUM
HAZING	VAGUELY	WISTFUL	WAN	REPUTATION

Speak Vocabulary

SENSIBILITIES	MALADJUSTED	PSEUDO	REFURBISHED	BIGOTED
SUBJECTIVITY	COAXES	RECESSIVE	INCRIMINATE	FLOUNDERING
DRONE	DORMANT	FREE SPACE	PRUNING	SANCTUARY
LEPER	MUSE	XENOPHOBIC	CONSISTENCY	DEMURE
DELINQUENCY	DYNAMICS	RETREAT	VESPIARY	ALLEGEDLY

Speak Vocabulary

CONUNDRUM	SENSIBILITIES	RECESSIVE	ALLEGEDLY	INCONSPICUOUS
MALADJUSTED	REFURBISHED	REPUTATION	BIGOTED	ASPHYXIATED
VAGUELY	GENETICS	FREE SPACE	MOMENTUM	RELUCTANCE
DELINQUENCY	DENSE	MUSE	TENACIOUS	XENOPHOBIC
IMBECILES	RETREAT	PRUNING	DEVIOUS	INDOCTRINATION

Speak Vocabulary

CONSISTENCY	DEGRADING	INCRIMINATE	REVOLUTIONARY	FLOUNDERING
WAN	COAXES	CONSCIENCE	SUBJECTIVITY	PSEUDO
HAZING	DEMERIT	FREE SPACE	FOSTER	DEMURE
LEPER	WISTFUL	BURROW	SANCTUARY	VESPIARY
DRONE	BANISHED	ERRANT	DORMANT	INCITING

Speak Vocabulary

GENETICS	PRUNING	INCRIMINATE	RETREAT	BIGOTED
CONSCIENCE	CONSISTENCY	SUBMISSION	XENOPHOBIC	CONUNDRUM
DRONE	WAN	FREE SPACE	SUBJECTIVITY	DENSE
PSEUDO	IMBECILES	INDOCTRINATION	REFURBISHED	DEGRADING
ASPHYXIATED	TENACIOUS	INCITING	DEMERIT	WISTFUL

Speak Vocabulary

RECESSIVE	SENSIBILITIES	ALLEGEDLY	REVOLUTIONARY	COAXES
VAGUELY	MALADJUSTED	VESPIARY	DELINQUENCY	BURROW
DEVIOUS	RELUCTANCE	FREE SPACE	ERRANT	FOSTER
DYNAMICS	SANCTUARY	FLOUNDERING	DEMURE	MUSE
DORMANT	BANISHED	MOMENTUM	LEPER	INCONSPICUOUS

Speak Vocabulary

DYNAMICS	INCITING	DEMERIT	ERRANT	LEPER
WISTFUL	FOSTER	GENETICS	MOMENTUM	INDOCTRINATION
REFURBISHED	REPUTATION	FREE SPACE	PSEUDO	CONUNDRUM
DEVIOUS	DORMANT	HAZING	MALADJUSTED	RETREAT
XENOPHOBIC	VAGUELY	SANCTUARY	DEGRADING	INCONSPICUOUS

Speak Vocabulary

ASPHYXIATED	INCRIMINATE	ALLEGEDLY	MUSE	DELINQUENCY
BANISHED	BURROW	RELUCTANCE	CONSCIENCE	DEMURE
DENSE	COAXES	FREE SPACE	BIGOTED	REVOLUTIONARY
SENSIBILITIES	SUBMISSION	CONSISTENCY	PRUNING	FLOUNDERING
DRONE	SUBJECTIVITY	VESPIARY	RECESSIVE	IMBECILES

Speak Vocabulary

BURROW	REVOLUTIONARY	ALLEGEDLY	SENSIBILITIES	XENOPHOBIC
INCITING	MUSE	DEMERIT	DYNAMICS	INCRIMINATE
HAZING	PRUNING	FREE SPACE	CONSISTENCY	BIGOTED
MALADJUSTED	VESPIARY	TENACIOUS	DRONE	RELUCTANCE
CONSCIENCE	SUBMISSION	DEGRADING	ASPHYXIATED	BANISHED

Speak Vocabulary

RECESSIVE	IMBECILES	REPUTATION	DEMURE	RETREAT
DEVIOUS	LEPER	COAXES	ERRANT	VAGUELY
WISTFUL	INCONSPICUOUS	FREE SPACE	DORMANT	INDOCTRINATION
GENETICS	CONUNDRUM	REFURBISHED	SANCTUARY	DENSE
WAN	MOMENTUM	DELINQUENCY	PSEUDO	FOSTER

Speak Vocabulary

REPUTATION	PRUNING	WISTFUL	DRONE	VESPIARY
MALADJUSTED	DEMURE	CONSCIENCE	XENOPHOBIC	WAN
DYNAMICS	HAZING	FREE SPACE	PSEUDO	DEMERIT
RETREAT	DEGRADING	GENETICS	SANCTUARY	CONSISTENCY
COAXES	INCONSPICUOUS	BURROW	BIGOTED	MUSE

Speak Vocabulary

INCRIMINATE	DENSE	DORMANT	VAGUELY	BANISHED
ASPHYXIATED	REFURBISHED	DELINQUENCY	RELUCTANCE	SUBMISSION
RECESSIVE	SUBJECTIVITY	FREE SPACE	INCITING	FOSTER
INDOCTRINATION	LEPER	SENSIBILITIES	FLOUNDERING	ERRANT
MOMENTUM	CONUNDRUM	DEVIOUS	ALLEGEDLY	TENACIOUS

Speak Vocabulary

IMBECILES	CONSCIENCE	INCRIMINATE	SANCTUARY	RECESSIVE
DYNAMICS	GENETICS	FLOUNDERING	DELINQUENCY	ERRANT
BURROW	REVOLUTIONARY	FREE SPACE	CONUNDRUM	INCONSPICUOUS
RETREAT	XENOPHOBIC	SUBMISSION	LEPER	DEMURE
ALLEGEDLY	RELUCTANCE	SUBJECTIVITY	COAXES	PSEUDO

Speak Vocabulary

MOMENTUM	DEGRADING	WAN	FOSTER	BIGOTED
PRUNING	REPUTATION	ASPHYXIATED	BANISHED	MUSE
TENACIOUS	DEVIOUS	FREE SPACE	REFURBISHED	VESPIARY
VAGUELY	WISTFUL	SENSIBILITIES	HAZING	MALADJUSTED
INCITING	DEMERIT	CONSISTENCY	DENSE	DORMANT

Speak Vocabulary

ERRANT	VESPIARY	LEPER	WAN	CONSISTENCY
PRUNING	HAZING	REVOLUTIONARY	VAGUELY	INCONSPICUOUS
REFURBISHED	COAXES	FREE SPACE	RELUCTANCE	FOSTER
INDOCTRINATION	SUBJECTIVITY	TENACIOUS	CONUNDRUM	DEMERIT
ASPHYXIATED	PSEUDO	WISTFUL	REPUTATION	SENSIBILITIES

Speak Vocabulary

DEMURE	CONSCIENCE	DELINQUENCY	RETREAT	XENOPHOBIC
MOMENTUM	IMBECILES	SUBMISSION	DORMANT	ALLEGEDLY
MUSE	SANCTUARY	FREE SPACE	MALADJUSTED	DRONE
INCITING	BURROW	GENETICS	FLOUNDERING	DENSE
BIGOTED	RECESSIVE	DYNAMICS	BANISHED	DEGRADING

Speak Vocabulary

PRUNING	DEGRADING	ASPHYXIATED	ERRANT	DEVIOUS
REFURBISHED	LEPER	DELINQUENCY	DEMERIT	WAN
SENSIBILITIES	FLOUNDERING	FREE SPACE	DORMANT	REPUTATION
SUBJECTIVITY	INCITING	INCONSPICUOUS	RECESSIVE	BIGOTED
REVOLUTIONARY	GENETICS	COAXES	ALLEGEDLY	SANCTUARY

Speak Vocabulary

HAZING	WISTFUL	SUBMISSION	BANISHED	DYNAMICS
CONSCIENCE	CONSISTENCY	INCRIMINATE	TENACIOUS	MALADJUSTED
RELUCTANCE	RETREAT	FREE SPACE	FOSTER	VESPIARY
BURROW	DRONE	INDOCTRINATION	DEMURE	PSEUDO
CONUNDRUM	VAGUELY	MUSE	MOMENTUM	DENSE

Speak Vocabulary

SUBMISSION	DEVIOUS	CONUNDRUM	DEMERIT	BANISHED
DYNAMICS	CONSISTENCY	MOMENTUM	FOSTER	VAGUELY
ALLEGEDLY	SANCTUARY	FREE SPACE	VESPIARY	IMBECILES
RECESSIVE	BIGOTED	CONSCIENCE	RELUCTANCE	BURROW
RETREAT	DENSE	ASPHYXIATED	SUBJECTIVITY	INCONSPICUOUS

Speak Vocabulary

FLOUNDERING	LEPER	DELINQUENCY	PSEUDO	GENETICS
DEMURE	WAN	REPUTATION	DEGRADING	XENOPHOBIC
REVOLUTIONARY	WISTFUL	FREE SPACE	REFURBISHED	MUSE
INCRIMINATE	DRONE	ERRANT	COAXES	MALADJUSTED
DORMANT	PRUNING	HAZING	INDOCTRINATION	INCITING

Speak Vocabulary

WAN	LEPER	SUBJECTIVITY	FLOUNDERING	PRUNING
VESPIARY	SUBMISSION	DYNAMICS	VAGUELY	BURROW
DRONE	RELUCTANCE	FREE SPACE	DORMANT	INCITING
INCRIMINATE	RECESSIVE	ASPHYXIATED	REFURBISHED	GENETICS
SANCTUARY	TENACIOUS	ALLEGEDLY	HAZING	REVOLUTIONARY

Speak Vocabulary

FOSTER	XENOPHOBIC	MOMENTUM	MALADJUSTED	DENSE
MUSE	INDOCTRINATION	WISTFUL	DEMURE	INCONSPICUOUS
ERRANT	REPUTATION	FREE SPACE	BIGOTED	CONSISTENCY
RETREAT	CONUNDRUM	DEVIOUS	BANISHED	DELINQUENCY
DEGRADING	SENSIBILITIES	COAXES	DEMERIT	CONSCIENCE

Speak Vocabulary

WISTFUL	DENSE	ERRANT	CONUNDRUM	DORMANT
CONSISTENCY	LEPER	SANCTUARY	SENSIBILITIES	BIGOTED
DEVIOUS	VAGUELY	FREE SPACE	SUBMISSION	DEMURE
BANISHED	RECESSIVE	ALLEGEDLY	VESPIARY	DEMERIT
COAXES	MALADJUSTED	MOMENTUM	PRUNING	WAN

Speak Vocabulary

DEGRADING	INCONSPICUOUS	IMBECILES	ASPHYXIATED	MUSE
INCITING	XENOPHOBIC	GENETICS	REPUTATION	DYNAMICS
INDOCTRINATION	BURROW	FREE SPACE	INCRIMINATE	RELUCTANCE
DELINQUENCY	HAZING	REFURBISHED	FLOUNDERING	PSEUDO
TENACIOUS	FOSTER	SUBJECTIVITY	CONSCIENCE	REVOLUTIONARY